OXFORD PROGRESSIVE ENGLISH READERS

General Editor: D. H. Howe

Wuthering Heights

Wuthering Heights

by EMILY BRONTË

HONG KONG

OXFORD UNIVERSITY PRESS

KUALA LUMPUR SINGAPORE JAKARTA TOKYO

Oxford University Press

OXFORD LONDON GLASGOW
NEW YORK TORONTO MELBOURNE WELLINGTON
KUALA LUMPUR SINGAPORE JAKARTA HONG KONG TOKYO
DELHI BOMBAY CALCUTTA MADRAS KARACHI
IBADAN NAIROBI DAR ES SALAAM CAPE TOWN

© *Oxford University Press 1975*
Second impression 1978

ISBN 0 19 580733 2

Retold by G.F. Wear. Illustrated by Poon Wai. Simplified according to the language grading scheme especially compiled by D.H. Howe.

Printed by Dai Nippon Printing Co. (H.K.) Ltd., 1 Pat Tat Street, Kowloon, Hong Kong
Published by Oxford University Press, News Building, North Point, Hong Kong

Contents

Oxford Progressive English Readers Language Scheme

The OPER language grading scheme was especially compiled by D. H. Howe as a guide to the preparation of language teaching material for school pupils and adults learning English as a second or foreign language. The scheme provides lists of words and language structures subdivided into three grades of difficulty and meant to be used in conjunction with each other.

The items were chosen according to two main principles: first, that they are likely to have been learnt or at least encountered *before* the stage indicated; second, that they are frequently occurring and useful, necessary to express a wide range of ideas, and difficult to replace with simpler words or constructions.

Use of the scheme is intended to eliminate unnecessary difficulties of language which would otherwise hinder understanding and enjoyment.

Introduction

Emily Brontë, the author of *Wuthering Heights,* was born in Yorkshire, in the North of England, in 1818. She was the fifth of six children. Two elder sisters, Maria and Elizabeth, died young in 1825. Her other two sisters were Charlotte and Anne, who were both well-known authors too. There was also a brother, Branwell, born in 1817. They were the children of a clergyman, the Rev. Patrick Brontë.

Their home was a wild, lonely house on the West Yorkshire moors. The Brontë children spent most of their lives there. There were no amusements for the girls, and no companions other than their own family. They depended on each other, and on books, to an extent that no child would do today. Their mother died in 1821, when they were all very young.

The three girls all wrote poetry and novels. *Wuthering Heights* was Emily's only novel. Many consider it to be the greatest of the Brontë novels. It was published in 1847.

The children inherited tuberculosis* from their mother, and all died young. Charlotte died at 39, Emily at 30, and Anne at 29.

The reader will find useful the relationship table on the following page. There are many people in the story with similar names, belonging to three generations of two families.

tuberculosis, a lung disease.

THE PEOPLE IN THE STORY

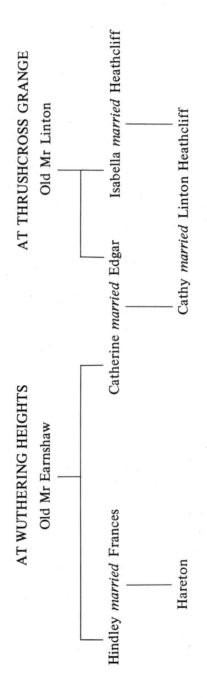

AT WUTHERING HEIGHTS

Old Mr Earnshaw

Hindley *married* Frances   Catherine *married* Edgar

Hareton

AT THRUSHCROSS GRANGE

Old Mr Linton

Isabella *married* Heathcliff

Cathy *married* Linton Heathcliff

Joseph,   a servant at Wuthering Heights.
Ellen Dean,   a servant, first at Wuthering Heights, then at
       Thrushcross Grange. She tells the story.
Zillah,   a servant at Wuthering Heights.

1   Heathcliff's Arrival

Before I came to live here at Thrushcross Grange, said Ellen
Dean, I was nearly always at Wuthering Heights. My mother
was employed there as a children's nurse, and I was allowed
to play with the two children, Hindley and Catherine. I liked
to do small jobs, too, and waited around the farm, ready for   5
anything that anybody would give me to do.

One fine summer morning at the beginning of the harvest,
in 1771 I think it was, Mr Earnshaw, the old master, came
downstairs dressed for a journey. First he told Joseph, the
servant, what was to be done during the day. Then he turned   10
to Hindley and Cathy. Speaking to his son, he said, 'Now, my
young man, I'm going to Liverpool today. What shall I bring
back for you? You may choose what you like, but it must be
small, for I shall walk there and back. It's sixty miles each
way, and that's a long distance.'   15

Hindley chose a fiddle*. Then the master asked Miss Cathy.
She was not quite six years old but she could ride any horse
in the stable, and she chose a whip. He did not forget me, for,
although he was rather severe sometimes, he had a kind heart.
He promised to bring me some apples and pears. Then he said   20
goodbye to his wife, kissed his children and set off.

It seemed a long time to us all — the three days that he was
away. Little Cathy often asked when her father would be
home. Mrs Earnshaw expected her husband by supper-time
on the third evening. Although we ate our meal late, there   25
was no sign of him coming. The children asked if they could
stay up and wait for him. Then, at last, at about eleven
o'clock, the door opened quietly and the master stepped in.
He threw himself into a chair. He looked tired and happy,
and told the children to wait patiently, for he was exhausted*   30
by his long walk.

*fiddle, musical instrument.
*exhausted, very tired.

'At the end of it, I was almost worried to death!' he said, opening his coat, which he held bundled up in his arms. 'Look! I have never been bothered so much by anything before. But you must take him as a gift of God.'

The strange child

We crowded round. Over Miss Cathy's head, I saw a dirty, 5
black-haired boy, big enough to walk and talk. Indeed, his face looked older than Catherine's. When he was set on his feet, he only stared round, and repeated some words that nobody could understand. I was frightened. What would they do with such a wild, dirty child? 10

The master tried to explain that he had pitied the child and decided to give him shelter under his own roof. He told us, quickly, that he had seen the child dying of hunger, homeless, and unable to speak any known language, in the streets of Liverpool. He had picked up the child and asked for his 15 owner. Nobody knew who owned the boy. Since the master had little money or time, he thought he should take the child home with him at once, because he was determined not to leave him where he had found him.

Mr Earnshaw then told me to wash the child, and give him 20 clean clothes and let him sleep with the children.

Hindley and Cathy were content to just look and listen until there was peace again. Then they both began searching their father's pockets for the presents he had promised them. Hindley was a boy of fourteen, but when he drew out what 25 had once been a fiddle, now crushed to pieces in his father's coat, he cried loudly. When Cathy heard that the master had lost her whip while looking after the stranger, she made a nasty face at the boy and spat at him. Her father then hit her, to teach her better manners. 30

The children refused to share a bed with him, or even to allow him in their room. I did not want him either, so I put him near the top of the stairs, hoping that he would be gone by the next day. In the night, the child crept to Mr Earnshaw's door. The master found him there the next day and asked 35 why he was there. I had to confess, and as a punishment for my cruel behaviour, I was sent out of the house.

    I went back a few days later, for I thought Mr Earnshaw did not want me to stay away for ever. I found they had named the boy Heathcliff. It was the name of Mr Earnshaw's son who had died. It was the only name they gave him and it was used both as his first name and his last one.

    Miss Cathy and he were now very good friends, but Hindley hated him. I hated him too, and we treated him very badly.

The new child causes jealousy

    He seemed a silent, patient child, perhaps because he was used to bad treatment. He accepted Hindley's beatings without crying once. If I pinched him, he would just breathe deeply and open his eyes, as if he had hurt himself by accident. Hindley's behaviour made old Mr Earnshaw very angry. When he discovered his son hurting Heathcliff, he always sympathized with Heathcliff and punished Hindley. It is true that Hindley was usually to blame. The master loved this stranger far more than he loved his own daughter, who was too naughty and mischievous to be a favourite.

    So from the beginning Heathcliff caused bad feeling in the house. When Mrs Earnshaw died, less than two years later, Hindley had already learnt to think of his father as a stern, unfriendly person rather than a loving father. Heathcliff was treated like a favourite son, and Hindley hated him more and more. He thought that this strange child had taken away all his father's love for his own son. I too often wondered why my master admired this unfriendly boy so much. I never saw him show any sign of real love towards Mr Earnshaw, for all his kindness.

    Then when the children fell ill with measles*, I had to look after them. It was then that my feelings changed towards Heathcliff. He was dangerously ill and I had to nurse him all the time. He was the quietest child anyone could have nursed, and he seemed grateful for my help. The difference between him and the other children made me like Heathcliff better.

*measles, children's disease which causes fever.

Heathcliff recovered, and the doctor praised me for caring for him so well. This pleased me greatly, and I became fond of Heathcliff, who had caused me to receive such praise. That was how Hindley lost his last supporter against Heathcliff.

2　The Death of Mr Earnshaw

In a few more years, old Mr Earnshaw began to grow weaker. He had been active and healthy, but his strength left him suddenly. He became unable to move about freely, and had to spend all his time in a chair. This made him extremely dif-
5 ficult, and he always became very bad-tempered if anyone did or said anything against Heathcliff. Nothing and nobody could please him except for his favourite. He seemed to believe that, because he liked Heathcliff, everyone else hated him and wanted to hurt him.
10　　Once or twice Hindley could not control himself and tried to injure Heathcliff in front of his father. The old man would become furious and try to beat Hindley with his stick, and when he found he was not strong enough to do so, he would shake with rage.
15　　At last it was feared that if this continued, the old man would kill himself. So Hindley was sent away to college, though his father thought that Hindley would never do well at anything.

I hoped that when Hindley had gone, we should have some
20 peace. We might have done, except for two people − Miss Cathy and the servant Joseph. Joseph was, and probably still is, the most unpleasant Bible-reading person alive. From the Bible he would find passages to prove himself always right and everyone else wrong. Because of his way with religion,
25 old Mr Earnshaw liked Joseph. The weaker the master became, the more influence Joseph gained. He was always talking to the master about his soul and about treating the children firmly. He encouraged the master to think badly of his son, and night after night he told hundreds of tales against
30 Catherine and Heathcliff. He was always careful that he put the heaviest blame for these things on Catherine, knowing that the master hated Heathcliff to be in the wrong.

Catherine

Certainly Catherine behaved as I never saw a child behave before. She caused so much trouble every day, making us all lose our patience more often than I could count. From the time she came downstairs from her bedroom in the morning, until she went to bed at night, we had no peace. Her spirits 5 were always high and she was always talking, singing, laughing and being a wild naughty thing. She was a wild and wicked thing, but she had the sweetest smile. And after all, I believe she meant no harm. When she really did make me lose all patience, she stopped her noise and quietly comforted me.　10

She was much too fond of Heathcliff. The greatest punishment we could invent for her was to keep her away from him. She got into more trouble over him than any of us.

In play, she liked more than anything else to act as a leader, using her hands freely, and commanding her companions. She 15 did so to me, but I would not let her slap me or give me orders. She soon learned not to play this game with me.

She used to tease her father terribly, not realising that his weakened health had changed him. She would do what he hated most, showing that she had more power over Heathcliff 20 than he did, in spite of his kindness. The boy would do anything she told him to do, but with old Mr Earnshaw he would only do what he wanted.

After behaving as badly as possible all day, she sometimes came to make it up at night.　25

'No, Cathy,' the old man would say, 'I cannot love you, you are worse than your brother. Go and say your prayers, child, and ask God's pardon.'

The master dies suddenly

But the day came at last that ended Mr Earnshaw's troubles on earth. He died quietly in his chair one October evening, 30 seated by the fireside.

A high wind blew round the house, and roared in the chimney. It sounded wild and stormy, yet it was not cold. We were all together inside. I sat a little away from the fire,

busy with my knitting. Joseph was reading his Bible near the table, (for the servants generally sat in the house then, after their work was finished). Miss Cathy had been ill, and that made her quiet. She was leaning against her father's knee, and
5 Heathcliff was lying on the floor with his head in her lap.

I remember the master, before he fell asleep, stroking her hair. It pleased him to see her gentle, and he said, 'Why can't you always be a good girl, Cathy?'

Cathy smiled and said she would sing her father to sleep.
10 She began singing very low, till his fingers dropped from hers, and his head sank on his chest. Then I told her to stop, for I feared she would wake him. We all kept very quiet for a full half-hour, and then it was time for Cathy to go to bed.

Joseph told the children to go upstairs and say their prayers.
15 'I shall say good-night to father first,' she said, putting her arms round his neck. The poor child discovered her loss immediately. She screamed out, 'Oh, he's dead, Heathcliff! He's dead!'

And they both started to cry, heartbroken.

Hindley brings home a wife
20 Mr Hindley, who had been away at college for three years, came home for the funeral. He did something that amazed us, and started the neighbours talking right and left – he brought a wife with him.

He never told us what she was and where she was born.
25 Probably Frances – that was her name – had neither family nor money to recommend her, or Hindley would surely have told his father about his marriage.

She was rather thin, but young and fresh. Her eyes shone like diamonds. She hated the funeral, and when I asked her
30 what the matter was she said, 'I don't know, but I am so afraid of dying!'

I did not think that she was likely to die. I did notice, however, that climbing the stairs made her breathe very quickly, and that she coughed badly sometimes. At the time
35 I did not know what these things meant. I certainly did not

intend to sympathize with her. We don't usually like foreigners
here, and any stranger was a foreigner to us.

Young Hindley Earnshaw had changed a lot in the three
years of his absence. He had grown thinner and lost his colour,
and spoke and dressed quite differently. On the very day of   5
his return he told Joseph and me that we must from then on
live in the back kitchen, and leave the main room for him and
his wife. Indeed, his wife liked the room very much. She expressed great pleasure in the white floor and huge glowing
fireplace, and the wide space to move about in, for the room   10
was very large.

She expressed pleasure, too, at finding a sister at Wuthering
Heights. She talked to Catherine, and played with her, ran
around with her and gave her presents from the very beginning. Her pleasure did not last long, however. When she grew   15
tired and unpleasant, Hindley became angry with everyone,
especially the person whom he blamed for her tiredness.

Heathcliff must live with servants

Heathcliff was the worst offender. When Frances told
Hindley how much she disliked the boy, Hindley remembered
his old hatred of Heathcliff. He told Heathcliff that he must   20
live with the servants, stopped his lessons, and insisted that
he must work on the farm instead, making him work as hard
as any other boy employed on the farm.

Heathcliff accepted all this fairly well at first, because
Cathy taught him what she learned, and worked or played   25
with him in the fields. The young master Hindley did not
seem to care how they grew up, how they behaved, or what
they did, so they became very wild. Nor did Hindley care
whether they went to church on Sundays. But Joseph and the
priest talked to him sternly about his duty to Catherine. When   30
he did think about the children, he ordered a beating for
Heathcliff and some kind of punishment for Catherine, like
sending her to her room with no supper.

One of their chief amusements was to run away to the
moors* in the morning and to stay there all day. They never   35
*moor, grassy area of open country where no crops grow.

worried about the punishment that usually followed, they only laughed at it. The priest could set as many chapters as he pleased for Catherine to learn by heart (he was her teacher), and Joseph could beat Heathcliff till his arm ached. They
5 forgot everything the minute they were together again.

One Sunday evening, they were sent from the sitting-room for making a noise, and when I went to call them to supper I could find them nowhere. We searched all over the house, and the yard and the stables. They seemed to have disappeared
10 completely. Hindley was very angry, and at last told us to lock the doors, and told us that no one was to let them in that night. Everyone went to bed, but I was too anxious to lie down. I opened my window and put my head out to listen. It was raining hard and I was determined to let them in when
15 they returned, although my master had told me not to.

Heathcliff returns alone

After a while, I heard steps coming up the road, and the light of a lamp shone at the gate. I threw a scarf over my head, and ran to the gate to prevent them from knocking and so waking up Mr Earnshaw. Heathcliff was standing there by
20 himself. It frightened me to see him alone.

'Where's Miss Catherine?' I cried. 'No accident, I hope?'

'At Thrushcross Grange,' he answered, 'and I should be there too. But they did not have enough manners to ask me to stay.'

25 'Well, you will be in trouble!' I said. 'You'll never be content until they send you away from here. Why did you wander to Thrushcross Grange?'

'Let me get off my wet clothes,' he replied, 'and I'll tell you all about it, Nelly.'

30 I warned him to be careful not to wake the master, and he continued, 'Cathy and I escaped from the wash-house so that we could run and be free. We noticed the lights of Thrushcross Grange, and we thought we would see whether the Lintons passed their Sunday evenings standing in corners for being
35 naughty while their father and mother sat eating and drinking

happily before the fire, as is the case here at Wuthering Heights.'

'They are good children, no doubt,' I said, 'and don't deserve the treatment you receive for your bad conduct.'

'That's nonsense, Nelly! We ran from the top of the Heights 5 to the Grange without stopping. We crept through a broken hedge, and found our way up to the path. Then we stood on top of a flowerpot under the sitting room window, where the light came from. They hadn't closed the curtains. We saw inside — ah! it was beautiful — a lovely place with red carpets 10 and red chairs. Old Mr and Mrs Linton were not there. Edgar and his sister were alone. They should have been happy, shouldn't they? We would have thought ourselves in heaven! And guess what those "good" children were doing. I believe Isabella is eleven, a year younger than Cathy. She lay scream- 15 ing at the farther end of the room. Edgar stood near the fire weeping silently, and in the middle of the table sat a little dog, shaking its paw and crying. We could see that they had nearly pulled the dog in two between them. The stupid things! That was their pleasure, to quarrel about who should hold 20 the dog, and to cry afterwards because both refused to take it. We laughed at them. We did think they were stupid. I would never wish to have what Cathy wanted. We would never amuse ourselves by yelling and sobbing, and rolling on the ground. I wouldn't want to exchange my life here, dif- 25 ficult though it is, for Edgar Linton's at Thrushcross Grange. Although I wish I could throw Joseph off the highest roof, or paint the front of the house with Hindley's blood!'

'Hush, hush!' I interrupted. 'You still have not told me, Heathcliff, why Catherine isn't with you.' 30

The dog bites Catherine

'I told you we laughed,' he answered. 'The Lintons heard us and rushed to the door. There was a silence and then a cry, "O Mamma, Mamma! O Papa! O Mamma, come here." We made terrible noises to frighten them still more, then we drop- ped down because someone was opening the front door, and 35

we felt we had better run. I was holding Cathy's hand, when she fell down suddenly. "Run, Heathcliff, run!" she whispered. "They have let the dog loose, and he is biting me!" The dog had seized her ankle, Nelly! She did not scream. She would
5 have been ashamed to do so. I did, though. I swore, and got a stone and forced it between the dog's teeth, but it would not let go. A servant came up with a lamp, shouting, "Keep hold, Skulker, keep hold!"

'He changed his order, however, when he saw that Skulker
10 was biting a girl. The dog was dragged off, blood pouring from his teeth. The man picked Cathy up and carried her into the house. She was sick — not from fear, I'm certain — but from pain. I followed, threatening the man if any harm should come to Cathy.
15   ' "What did he catch, Robert?" shouted Mr Linton from the doorway.

    ' "Skulker has caught a little girl, sir," he replied. "And there's a boy here as well," he added. "Very likely the robbers were going to make them climb through the window, to open
20 the doors to the gang* after everyone had gone to sleep." Then he turned to me, and shaking my arm, said, "Hold your tongue, you thief! You shall hang for this! Mr Linton, sir, keep your gun by you!"

    ' "Well Robert," said the old man, "the gang must have
25 known that yesterday was my rent-day. They wanted to take all the money I have collected. Come in. Fasten the chain. Give Skulker some water." And to his wife he added, "Oh, my dear Mary, look here! Don't be afraid, it's only a boy. Yet I agree he has a horrible face. It would be a kindness to
30 the country to hang him at once, before he does something worse."

'He pulled me under the light, and the cowardly children crept nearer.

    ' "Frightful thing," said Isabella. "Put him in the cellar,
35 Papa!"

'While they examined me, Cathy recovered and heard the last part of this speech. She laughed. Edgar Linton looked up
*gang, group of bad people.

at her quickly, and recognized her. "That's Miss Earnshaw," he whispered to his mother, "I've seen her in church."

'His mother didn't believe him. "Miss Earnshaw? Nonsense! Miss Earnshaw running around the country with a half wild boy? Yet this child is in black — for her dead father perhaps?   *5* Surely it is her."

' "What a disgraceful lack of responsibility her brother must have!" exclaimed Mr Linton. "But who is this with her? I know," he said excitedly, "it's that strange child he found on that trip to Liverpool — a little Indian, or an American, or   *10* Spanish child."

' "A wicked boy, anyway," remarked the old lady. "And not fit for a decent house! Did you notice his language, Linton? I'm shocked that my children should have heard it."

Heathcliff is sent away

'I started swearing again — don't be angry Nelly — and so   *15* Robert was ordered to see that I left immediately. I refused to go without Cathy, so he dragged me into the garden. He pushed the lamp into my hand, and told me that Mr Earnshaw would be informed of my behaviour. He ordered me to start on my journey home, and fastened the door again.   *20*

'The curtains were still open at one end, so I started watching again. If Catherine had wanted to return, I would have broken their big window into a million pieces, if they had not let her out.

'Catherine was sitting on the sofa quietly. Mrs Linton took   *25* off the maid's grey coat, which we had borrowed for our expedition. Then the woman servant brought a basin of warm water, and washed her feet. Mr Linton mixed her some kind of warm drink. Isabella gave her some cakes, and Edgar stood staring at a distance. Afterwards they dried her beautiful hair,   *30* and gave her a pair of enormous house-shoes. They put her in front of the fire where she happily combed her hair, dividing her food between the little dog and Skulker.

'She was a young lady, and so they treated her and me differently. She was quite happy, and so I left her and returned   *35* here, Nelly.'

'More will come of this business than you think,' I said. 'You have behaved badly Heathcliff, and Mr Hindley will punish you harshly for this.'

The unfortunate adventure made Hindley very angry. Mr
5 Linton visited us the next day, and gave the master a lecture on the way he was looking after his family. Mr Hindley decided on a cruel punishment. Heathcliff received no beating, but he was told that if he ever spoke to Miss Catherine again he would be sent away from the house. Mrs Earnshaw
10 decided to look after Catherine more carefully than before. She would use kindness on Catherine when she returned home, not force. She could never have achieved anything with Catherine by force.

3 A Lady Returns to Wuthering Heights

Cathy stayed at Thrushcross Grange for five weeks, till Christmas. By that time, her ankle was completely healed, and her manners were greatly improved. The mistress visited her often. She started her plan of reform* by giving Cathy fine clothes and telling her how pretty she looked in them. At last, when   *5* Cathy returned we saw, instead of a wild, hatless little savage jumping into the house, stepping down from a handsome black pony, a very dignified person, with brown curled hair falling from the cover of a feather hat. She wore a long riding dress which she had to hold up with both hands so that she   *10* could walk.

Mr Hindley lifted her from her pony, exclaiming delightedly, 'Why Cathy, you are quite a beauty! I should hardly have known you. You look like a lady now. Isabella Linton cannot be compared with her, can she Frances?'   *15*

'Isabella does not have her natural advantages,' replied his wife. 'But Catherine must be careful that she does not grow wild here again. Ellen, help Miss Catherine take off her things.'

I removed the hat, being careful not to spoil her hair, and took her coat. She looked lovely. Then the dogs ran up, but   *20* she hardly dared touch them, in case they should make her dirty.

She kissed me gently. I was covered in flour from making the Christmas cake, and she could not embrace me. Then she looked round for Heathcliff. Mr and Mrs Earnshaw watched   *25* anxiously for this meeting. They wanted to know if they would be able to separate the two friends.

Heathcliff has grown worse
Heathcliff was hard to find at first. He had become ten times more careless and uncared for while Catherine was away.   *30*

reform, to improve something bad.

I was the only one who called him dirty, and told him to wash himself. Children of his age seldom have a natural pleasure in soap and water. His clothes had been worn for three months in mud and dust. His hair was thick, dirty and uncombed and his face and hands were absolutely black. He hid   5
behind some furniture, when he saw a bright, graceful young lady enter the house instead of the rough playmate he expected.

'Isn't Heathcliff here?' she demanded, pulling off her gloves and showing fingers wonderfully whitened with doing nothing,   10
and staying indoors.

'Heathcliff, you may come forward,' cried Mr Hindley. 'You may come and wish Miss Catherine welcome like the other servants.'

Cathy saw her friend in his hiding place. She rushed towards   15
him and gave him seven or eight kisses on his cheek. Then she stopped, and drawing back, burst into a laugh, exclaiming, 'Why, how very black and angry you look! And how funny! But that's because I'm used to Edgar and Isabella Linton. Well, Heathcliff, have you forgotten me?'   20

She had good reason to ask the question. Shame and pride had made his expression very dark and serious, and kept him from moving to her.

'Shake hands, Heathcliff,' said Mr Earnshaw. 'Sometimes it is permitted.'   25

'I shall not,' replied the boy, at last able to speak. 'I shall not stay to be laughed at. I shall not!'

He tried to escape from us, but Miss Cathy seized him again.

'I did not mean to laugh at you,' she said. 'Heathcliff,   30
shake hands at least! Why are you angry? I only laughed because you looked so odd. If you wash your face, and brush your hair it will be all right. But you are so dirty!'

She looked sadly at the dirty fingers she held in her own, and also at her dress, which she feared had become dirty from   35
touching him.

'You needn't have touched me!' he answered, following

her eyes and taking away his hand. 'I shall be as dirty as I want. I like to be dirty, and I *shall* be dirty!'

With that, he rushed straight out of the room. The master and mistress were very amused, but Catherine could not
5 understand why her remarks had make him so angry.

When I had looked after Cathy, and put my cakes in the oven, I made the sitting room and kitchen cheerful with big fires. Then I sat down and remembered what it was like before at Christmas when old Mr Earnshaw was alive. He used to
10 give me a shilling as a Christmas present. Then I thought of his fondness for Heathcliff, and his fear that he would suffer after his death. That naturally made me consider the poor boy's situation now, and I became very sad. But I realised that I should try to improve his position instead of crying for
15 him. So I got up to look for him. I knew that Miss Catherine had asked the Lintons to come over that day. I intended to make Heathcliff clean and tidy so that he need not be ashamed to meet them.

I found Heathcliff brushing one of the ponies in the stable.
20 It was Miss Cathy's new pony.

'Heathcliff,' I said, 'Cathy is very sad that she never sees you now. She cried when I told her you had run off to the moors again this morning.'

'Well, I cried last night,' he replied, 'and I had more reason
25 to cry than she.'

'Oh, Heathcliff, you are showing a poor spirit! Come to the mirror, and let me make you clean and tidy.'

The Lintons arrive

So we talked about this and that. Heathcliff began to look quite handsome as he gradually lost his frown and began to
30 smile. Suddenly our conversation was interrupted by a sound in the courtyard. Heathcliff ran to the window, and I to the door. We saw the two Lintons descending from the family carriage, and the Earnshaws getting down from their horses. Catherine took a hand of each of the Linton children, and
35 brought them into the house and sat them before the fire, which quickly put colour into their white faces.

I urged Heathcliff to hurry now and show a pleasant face. He seemed to obey, but unfortunately, when he opened the door leading from the kitchen on one side, Hindley opened the door on the other side. They met, and the master, annoyed at seeing Heathcliff clean, pushed him back angrily. He 5 told Joseph to keep him out of the room. Then he spoke to Heathcliff, 'Get out of here! Just wait till I get hold of you. I'll pull your hair till it stretches.'

'It is long enough already,' said Master Linton, looking through the doorway. 'I'm surprised that hair doesn't give 10 him a headache.'

I think he said that without intending to insult Heathcliff. But Heathcliff was so violent that he would not accept even the appearance of an insult from someone he hated, even then, as a rival. He seized a bowl of hot apple sauce from the 15 table, the first thing he could find, and threw it against Edgar Linton's face and neck. Edgar's cries brought Isabella and Catherine hurrying to him. Mr Earnshaw caught Heathcliff immediately and took him to his room, where he was almost beaten to death. 20

I got a cloth, and rather harshly washed Edgar's nose and mouth. His sister began crying and saying that she wanted to go home. Cathy stood nearby, upset by everything.

'You shouldn't have spoken to him!' she said excitedly. 'He was in a bad temper. Now you've spoilt your visit, and 25 he'll be beaten. I hate him to be beaten. I can't eat my dinner. Why did you speak to him, Edgar?'

'I didn't,' cried the boy, escaping from my hands. 'I promised Mamma that I wouldn't say one word to him, and I didn't.' 30

'Well don't cry,' replied Catherine harshly. 'You're not dead. Don't make any more mischief. My brother is coming. Be quiet! Hush, Isabella! No one has hurt you!'

'Never mind, children, sit down,' said Hindley, walking in with a smile. 'I have settled that terrible child nicely. Next 35 time, Master Edgar, use your own hands to fight him, it will make you enjoy your food even more.'

The little party became more cheerful at the sight of the feast laid out on the table. They were hungry after their ride, and cheered up easily since no real harm had happened to them. Mr Earnshaw gave them large amounts of food, and the
5   mistress made them laugh with lively talk. I stood behind her chair, and watched Catherine. At first, I didn't think she cared what had happened to Heathcliff. But I was wrong. She lifted a mouthful of food to her lips then put it down again. Her cheeks paled and tears fell. She dropped her fork on the
10 floor and hastily dived under the cloth to hide her emotion. I realised that she felt terrible about Heathcliff throughout the day. She was hoping to find an opportunity to visit him. where he had been locked up by the master.

In the evening we had a dance. Cathy asked if Heathcliff
15 could be freed then, as Isabella Linton had no partner. But she had no success. I had to dance instead. Our pleasure was increased by the arrival of the Gimmerton band. They go around to all the respectable houses at Christmas time. Mrs Earnshaw loved the music, and so they gave us plenty.

Catherine leaves the party
20   Catherine loved it too, but she said it sounded best at the top of the steps, and she went up in the dark. I followed, shutting the sitting room door as I went through. Nobody noticed our absence, there were too many people. Catherine did not stop at the top of the stairs, but climbed further, to
25 the room where Heathcliff had been put. She called him softly. At first he refused to answer, but in the end they were talking away happily. I allowed the poor things to continue until I thought the songs downstairs would have finished. Then I climbed up to warn them. Instead of finding her out-
30 side, I heard her voice inside. The naughty child had gone onto the roof, through one window, and down into Heath-cliff's room through another. It was very difficult for me to persuade her to come out. When she did, she brought Heath-cliff with her. She insisted that I should take him down to the
35 kitchen and give him some food. I replied that, as the prisoner

had not eaten since dinner the day before, I would not mind him cheating Mr Hindley just once.

We went down to the kitchen and I put him on a stool by the fire. But he was sick and could eat only a little. He leant his elbows on his knees and his chin on his hands. When I enquired what he was thinking about, he answered quietly and seriously.

'I'm trying to decide how I shall pay Hindley back. I don't care how long I wait, if I can only do it in the end. I hope he doesn't die before me!'

'For shame, Heathcliff!' I said. 'It is God's duty to punish wicked people. We should learn to forgive.'

'No,' he said. 'I only wish I knew the best way to do it. Leave me alone, and I'll plan it, don't worry. While I can plan how to do it, I don't feel any of the pain he causes me now.'

4 The Birth of Hareton

On the morning of a fine June day in 1778, Hareton, the last of the Earnshaws, was born. Mrs Earnshaw, however, did not live long. The doctor told my master, as soon as the child was born, that his wife was very ill. But he would not believe it.
5 He loved his wife deeply, the only person he did love, I'm sure. I didn't know how he would bear her death.

He told his wife there was nothing to worry about, and she seemed to believe him. But one night, she was leaning on his shoulder, and saying she thought she could get up the next
10 day. Suddenly, she started coughing slightly, and he raised her in his arms. She put her hands about his neck, her face changed, and she was dead.

The baby, Hareton, became my responsibility. As long as the child was healthy and Mr Earnshaw never heard him cry,
15 he was content to let him be cared for by others. He wanted nothing to do with the child whom he blamed for his wife's death.

Hindley Earnshaw became desperate. He did not cry or pray, but he swore, and shouted at everyone. In the end, the
20 other servants could not bear his terrible behaviour any longer. Joseph and I were the only two who would stay.

The master's bad ways and bad companions formed a dreadful example for Catherine and Heathcliff. And Heathcliff delighted to see Hindley become worse and worse. We
25 lived in a terrible house. The priest stopped visiting, and nobody came near us in the end, except Edgar Linton who came to see Miss Cathy.

Cathy grows up
At fifteen Cathy was the queen of the countryside. There was no one as beautiful as her, but she was a difficult person
30 to like. She always wanted her own way and could be very

rude. In fact, once her childhood was over, I must admit I didn't like her very much. She never took a dislike to me, though. She always remembered her old friends – even Heathcliff remained a close friend. Young Edgar Linton, in spite of his better position, found it difficult to make an 5 equally strong friend of her.

Catherine had continued her friendship with the Lintons since she had stayed with them. She did not show her rough side while she was with them. She behaved beautifully with the old Mr and Mrs Linton, and gained the admiration of 10 Isabella. She also gained the heart and soul of the brother, Edgar. She liked all this from the beginning, for she was full of ambition. In the end, she developed a double character, without meaning to deceive anyone. In the Lintons' house, where she heard Heathcliff called 'a terrible, rough lad' and 15 'worse than a beast', she took care not to act like him. But at home, at Wuthering Heights, she did not want to be polite, because she would only be laughed at. She did not need to hide her wild nature when it would not bring her praise.

Mr Edgar was not usually brave enough to visit Wuthering 20 Heights openly. He was terrified of Earnshaw's reputation, and did not want to meet him. But when he came we always did our best to be polite. The master, Mr Earnshaw, tried not to offend him, because he knew why he came. If he could not be well behaved, Mr Earnshaw tried to keep out of the 25 way. I think that Catherine did not really like Edgar's visits. She obviously did not like Heathcliff and Edgar to meet. I often laughed at how this used to worry her.

Mr Hindley had left home one afternoon, and because he was not there, Heathcliff decided to give himself a holiday. 30 He had reached the age of sixteen by then, I think. Although he was not stupid or ugly, he managed to appear both of these things. In the first place he had lost all the benefit of his early education. His continual hard work had made him lose any interest he had once had in knowledge, learning and 35 books. His childhood pride, which he had had because of old Mr Earnshaw's friendship, had disappeared completely. He

had long ago given up trying to follow Catherine in her studies, though one could see the silent regret. Nothing could make him take an interest in things outside himself. His physical appearance showed his mental lack of interest. He
5   no longer walked straight, but was bent and dragged his feet. He seemed to enjoy making all of his few companions dislike him.

Catherine and he were still constant companions when he was not working. But he tried to avoid her girlish admiration
10 as if he realised that she could no longer be good for him. On the afternoon just mentioned, he came into the house to tell us of his intention to take a holiday. I was helping Miss Cathy to dress and do her hair. She had not realised that Heathcliff would not be working that afternoon. Because she had
15 thought she would have the house to herself, she had managed to send a message to Mr Edgar, telling him of her brother's absence. She hoped that he would be able to come over and see her. Heathcliff's appearance was obviously going to cause trouble.

20   'Joseph will tell Hindley about this,' she said.

'Joseph is busy working elsewhere,' Heathcliff answered.

Catherine did not know what to do. Eventually she said, 'Isabella and Edgar Linton said they would visit this afternoon. If they come, you will be in trouble for no reason.'

25   'Tell Ellen to say that you are busy, Cathy,' he replied. 'Don't turn me away for those awful, silly friends of yours! You spend so much time with them, and so very little with me.'

'And why should I always sit with you?' she demanded,
30 growing more angry. 'What use is it? What do you talk about? You say and do nothing to amuse me!'

'You never told me before that I talked too little, or that you disliked my company, Cathy!' exclaimed Heathcliff, very upset.

35   'It's no company at all, when people know nothing and say nothing,' she muttered.

Heathcliff stood up, but he had no time to express his

feelings further. They heard a horse's feet outside, and young Linton knocked and entered.

Catherine quarrels with Edgar

Catherine noticed the difference between her two friends as one came in and the other walked out. The contrast was like changing a cold, hilly, coal country for a beautiful green *5* valley. Edgar's voice and greeting were totally opposite to Heathcliff's behaviour. Edgar had a quiet, pleasant way of speaking.

'I've not come too soon, have I?' he asked, looking at me. I had begun to tidy the room. *10*

'No,' answered Catherine. 'What are you doing there, Nelly?' She was obviously trying to get rid of me, but Mr Hindley had told me to stay with them during Linton's private visits.

She stepped behind me and whispered angrily, 'Go away, *15* Nelly. When there are visitors in the house, servants don't start dusting and cleaning in the room where they are!'

Then, thinking that Edgar could not see her, she pinched me, very hard, on the arm. I have said I did not love her. Besides she hurt me, and I screamed out, 'Oh, Miss, that's a *20* nasty trick! You have no right to pinch me!'

'I didn't touch you, you lying creature!' she cried, her ears red with rage. She could never hide her anger.

'What's that, then?' I demanded, showing the purple mark on my arm. *25*

She stamped her foot, and then slapped me on the cheek — a stinging blow that filled both my eyes with tears.

'Catherine, my dear, Catherine!' said Edgar Linton. He was greatly shocked at Cathy's behaviour. Shocked, both by her lies and by her violence. *30*

'Leave the room, Ellen!' she commanded, trembling all over.

Little Hareton was sitting near me on the floor. Seeing my tears, he started crying himself. Cathy seized his shoulders, and shook him till the poor child looked quite sick. Edgar *35*

without hesitating, tried to stop Catherine shaking the child. Immediately, Cathy's rage was directed towards him. She took hold of his ear, and shook his head in a way that could not be mistaken for a game. He drew back, with a puzzled
5 look on his face. I lifted Hareton in my arms, while no one was paying any attention to him, and walked off to the kitchen with him. I left the door open, for I was curious to see how they would settle their disagreement.

Edgar took up his hat and moved towards the front door.
10 'Where are you going?' demanded Catherine, advancing to the door.

He tried to pass her, without pushing her.

'You must not go!' she said.

'I must and I shall!' he replied, in a quiet but firm voice.
15 'Can I stay after you have treated me like that?'

Catherine was silent.

'You've made me afraid and ashamed of you,' he continued. 'I shall not come here again.'

Edgar comes back

Edgar walked quickly outside, then, he hesitated, and
20 looked back inside through the window. He was weak and looked inside.

Ah, I thought, he cannot be saved.

I was right. He turned quickly, and hurried into the house again and shut the door behind him. Later, I went in to in-
25 form them that Mr Hindley had come home very drunk and was likely to cause trouble. I saw that the quarrel had only made them closer.

However, when Linton heard that Mr Hindley had arrived, Linton rode off on his horse, and Catherine went to her room.
30 I went to hide little Hareton, and to empty the master's gun, for he liked to play with it when he was drunk. One day he would kill someone, if I forgot to unload his gun.

Hindley entered, shouting and swearing, and making a noise. He found me hiding his son away in the kitchen cup-
35 board. Hareton was terrified of his father, whether he showed

fondness or anger. When his father was showing his love, he
was in danger of being squeezed to death. When he was angry,
the child could be thrown into the fire, or against a wall. So,
the poor thing remained perfectly quiet, wherever I chose to
put him.   5

'There, I've found out at last!' cried Hindley, dragging me
back from the cupboard like a dog. 'You have decided between you to murder that child! Now I know why he is always out of my way. Hareton deserves beating for not running to welcome me, and for screaming as if I were the devil. 10
Now, don't you think the lad would look better if his hair
were shaved off? It makes a dog more fierce, and I love fierce
things. Get me some scissors! And he doesn't need ears, does
he? I'll take them off too. Hush, child, hush! Kiss me! What,
you won't? Hareton, if you won't kiss me, I'll break your   15
neck!'

Heathcliff saves Hareton's life

Poor Hareton was screaming and kicking in his father's
arms, and he shouted even louder when Hindley carried him
upstairs and lifted him over the rail. I cried out that he would
frighten the child to death, and ran to rescue him. As I   20
reached them, Hindley leant forward on the rails to listen to
a noise below. I recognised Heathcliff's steps. Then Hareton
gave a sudden struggle. Hindley was not paying enough attention, and after a moment, the child fell.

By the time I realised what had happened, the little thing 25
was safe. Heathcliff arrived underneath just at the right moment, and with a quick movement he caught Hareton. Putting
the child on its feet, he looked up to see who could have
caused such an accident. I rushed downstairs and held the
precious child to my heart. Hindley came down more slowly, 30
serious and ashamed.

'It is your fault, Ellen,' he said. 'You should have kept him
out of sight. Is he injured anywhere?'

'Injured!' I cried angrily. 'If he's not dead, he will be stupid
for the rest of his life! Oh, I am surprised that his mother 35

does not rise from the dead and see how you treat him! How can you treat your own child this way? You shall not touch him any more. He hates you, they all hate you, that's the truth! A happy family you have, and what a dreadful state
5   you have come to.'

'I shall get worse yet, Nelly,' laughed the terrible man, recovering his hardness. 'Now, take yourself and him out of my sight. And Heathcliff, you get out too, away from my reach and hearing. I won't try to murder you tonight, unless per-
10   haps I set the house on fire. It depends on my mood.'

He took a bottle of brandy* from the cupboard and poured some into a glass.

'No, don't,' I said, trying to take the glass from him. 'Mr Hindley, do take care. Have mercy on this unfortunate boy,
15   even if you care nothing for yourself!'

'Anyone can do better for him than I shall,' he answered.

He drank down the brandy, and impatiently told us to go.

'It's a pity he can't kill himself with drink,' said Heathcliff. 'He's doing his best, but he is too strong and healthy.'
20   I went into the kitchen and sat down to try and get the little child to sleep.

*brandy, a strong drink.

5 Heathcliff Runs Away

I was rocking Hareton to sleep on my knee, and singing a song. I thought that Heathcliff had gone through into the barn, but I found afterwards that he had only got as far as the sofa*. He had decided to stay inside, so he sat down on a bench, quite a long way from the fire, and remained silent.   *5*

Miss Cathy, who had been listening to all the noise from her room, put her head into the kitchen and whispered, 'Are you alone, Nelly?'

'Yes Miss,' I replied.

She entered and came close to the fire. The expression on   *10* her face was disturbed and anxious. Her lips were half open, as if she were going to speak. But, I had not forgotten her recent behaviour, and I started my song again, ignoring her.

'Where's Heathcliff?' she asked, interrupting me.

'At his work in the stable,' was my reply.   *15*

Heathcliff still did not speak, perhaps he had fallen asleep. Another pause followed.

'Oh dear!' said Catherine at last. 'I'm very unhappy!'

'A pity,' said I. 'You're difficult to please. You have so many friends, and so few worries, and you still can't be   *20* happy!'

Catherine has promised to marry Edgar

'Nelly, will you keep a secret for me?' she continued. She knelt down by me and lifted her eyes to my face, with the sort of look which always cured my bad temper.

'Is the secret worth keeping?' I asked in a more friendly   *25* voice.

'Yes, and it worries me, and I must tell someone. I want to know what I should do. Today Edgar Linton asked me to marry him, and I've given him an answer. Now, before I tell

*sofa, a large chair, big enough for several people to sit on.

you whether it was yes or not, you tell me what it should have been.'

'Really Miss Catherine, how can I know?' I replied. 'When I remember the way you behaved in front of him this after-
5 noon, I think you should have refused him. Since he asked you after that, he must either be hopelessly foolish or very stupid.'

'If you talk like that, I won't tell you any more. I accepted him, Nelly. Be quick, and say whether I was wrong.'
10 'You accepted him! Then what good is it discussing the matter? You have promised, and you can't change your mind now.'

'But say whether I should have done so – please.'

'There are many things to be considered,' I answered.
15 'First, and most important, do you love Mr Edgar?'

'Who can help it? Of course I do.'

'Why do you love him, Miss Cathy?'

'I do – that's a good enough reason.'

'No, it is not, you must say why.'
20 'Well, because he is handsome, and pleasant to be with. Because he is young and cheerful.'

'Bad!' was all I could say.

'And because he loves me and he will be rich. I shall enjoy being the greatest woman of the neighbourhood, and I shall
25 be proud of having such a husband.'

'Worst of all. You love Mr Edgar because he is handsome, young, cheerful, and rich, and loves you. He won't always be handsome and young, and may not always be rich.'

'He is now, and I am only worried about the present. I
30 wish you would tell me what you think.'

'Well, that decides the matter. If you are only thinking of the present, marry Mr Linton.'

'I don't want your permission – I shall marry him. I want to know if you think I'm right to do so.'
35 'Perfectly right, if it's right for people to marry only for the present. And now let's hear what you are unhappy about. Your brother will be pleased. Old Mr and Mrs Linton will not

object, I think. You will escape from a disorderly, uncomfortable home into a wealthy, respectable one. And you love Edgar and Edgar loves you. Everything seems smooth and easy. What is the matter?'

'Here, and here!' replied Catherine, striking one hand on 5
her forehead and the other over her heart, 'wherever the soul lives. In my soul and in my heart, I'm sure I'm wrong.'

'That's very strange. I don't understand.'

'This is my secret. Please don't laugh at me and I'll try to explain.' 10

She looked sad and serious. Her hands trembled.

'Nelly, do you ever dream strange dreams?'

'Yes, now and then.'

Catherine loves Heathcliff

'So do I. Many of them. I dreamt once that I was in heaven, but it did not seem to be my home. I broke my heart with 15
crying when I came back to earth. The angels were so angry with me that they threw me out into the middle of the moor above Wuthering Heights, where I woke up, full of joy. That will explain my secret. I've no more right to marry Edgar Linton than I have to be in heaven. If my wicked brother in 20
there had not treated Heathcliff so badly, I shouldn't have thought of it. But I cannot marry Heathcliff now, not while he is in his present position. So he shall never know how much I love him. And that is not because he is handsome, Nelly, but because he is more myself than I am. Whatever our 25
souls are made of, his and mine are the same. Linton's soul is as different as moonlight from lightning, or frost from fire.'

Before this speech had ended I realized that Heathcliff was in the room. Having noticed a slight movement, I turned my head, and saw him rise from the bench and creep out quietly. 30
He had listened till he had heard Catherine say that she could not marry him. Then he left without waiting to hear any more. Catherine, seated on the floor, did not see him.

'Nelly, don't you realize that if Heathcliff and I were to marry, we would be beggars? If I marry Edgar, I can help 35

Heathcliff to improve his position, and take him out of my brother's power.'

'With your husband's money, Miss Catherine? It won't be as easy as you think. I think that's the worst reason you've
5 given yet for marrying young Linton.'

'It is not,' she replied, 'it's the best! The others were for me or Edgar. This is for the sake of someone who understands. My love for Edgar is like the leaves of trees. Time will change them. But my love for Heathcliff is like the everlast-
10 ing rocks underneath. A cause for little visible delight, but necessary. Nelly, Heathcliff is always, always in my mind — not as a pleasure to myself, but as my own being. So don't talk of our separation. . . '

She paused, and hid her face in my skirt, but I moved her
15 away forcibly. I was angry with her.

'I can't really understand your nonsense, Miss,' I said. 'But I know that you do not understand the duties or purpose of marriage. Don't tell me any more secrets. I will not promise to keep them.'

20 'Will you keep the one I've just told you?' she asked eagerly.

'I can't promise,' I repeated.

Where is Heathcliff?

Just then, Joseph came in and we stopped talking. I whispered to Cathy that Heathcliff had heard a lot of our
25 conversation, and told her how I saw him leave the kitchen. She jumped up, looking very worried, and ran off to find her friend. She was absent such a long time that Joseph said that we shouldn't wait any longer. He thought that the two were staying out of the way until his prayers for the meal were
30 over. So he added an extra prayer on their behalf, to the usual fifteen minutes he took for these occasions. At the end of supper, young Cathy rushed into the kitchen and ordered him to hurry down the road and to find Heathcliff, wherever he was, and to make him return immediately.

35 'I want to speak to him, and I must, before I go to bed

tonight,' she said. 'The gate is open. He is somewhere out there, beyond hearing, because I shouted as loud as I could.'

Joseph objected at first, but at last he placed his hat on his head, and went out, muttering against women.

5   Catherine could not keep still.

'I wonder where he is,' she exclaimed. 'What did I say, Nelly? Tell me what I said to upset him. I do wish he'd come back.'

'What a bother about nothing!' I cried, though I also felt 10 rather worried, especially when Joseph returned alone.

'Have you found Heathcliff, you fool?' asked Catherine. 'Have you been looking for him as I ordered?'

'Indeed I have,' answered Joseph, 'and the stupid boy left the gate open. Your pony has got in among the flowers. I'll 15 do something terrible to him, when I find him, I tell you. It's very dark out there, I swear we'll have a storm tonight.'

It was a very dark evening for summer. The clouds were heavy and low. The approaching rain would bring Heathcliff home, we thought.

20   The rain came, but no Heathcliff. In the end, Cathy went out and stood near the road. She stayed there, not caring about the wind and rain, calling sometimes and then listening. She did not listen to my advice to wait inside.

At about midnight the storm came over the Heights in full 25 strength. There was a violent wind, as well as thunder. A tree at the corner of the building split in two. It knocked down part of the east chimney, sending stones and coal dust into the kitchen fire.

The storm passed away in twenty minutes, leaving us all 30 unharmed except Cathy, who got completely wet by standing hatless in the rain and refusing to take shelter. She came in and lay down on the sofa, with her clothes wet through.

'Well, Miss!' I said. 'Are you determined to die of cold? It's half past twelve. It is no good waiting any longer for the boy. 35 He must have gone to Gimmerton, and he'll stay there now.'

'No, I don't think he has reached Gimmerton,' said Joseph nastily, 'I expect he's at the bottom of some damp hole on the moor.'

I tried to get Catherine to rise and take off her wet things, but I had no success. I gave up, and went to bed taking little Hareton with me.

In the morning I came down and saw Catherine still seated near the fire-place. The door was open already. Hindley had *5* come down, and he was standing near the fire looking almost as bad as Catherine herself.

'What's the matter with you, Cathy?' he asked. 'You look like a drowned dog. Why are you so damp and pale, child?'

'I've been wet,' she answered slowly, 'and I'm cold, that's *10* all.'

'Oh, she is naughty!' I cried, seeing that the master wasn't drunk. 'She got wet in the rain yesterday evening, and there she has sat all through the night.'

Mr Earnshaw stared at us in surprise. 'All through the *15* night?' he repeated. 'What kept her up? Not fear of thunder, surely?'

Neither of us wanted to mention Heathcliff's absence as long as we could conceal it, so I replied that I didn't know, and she said nothing. *20*

Catherine is ill

I threw open the window, and filled the room with fresh, cool morning air, but Catherine called to me, shivering, 'Shut the window, Ellen, I'm cold.'

'She's ill,' said Hindley, taking her wrist. 'I suppose that's the reason she would not go to bed. I don't want to be *25* troubled with more sickness here. Why did you go into the rain?'

'Running after Heathcliff,' muttered Joseph, 'I expect she was with that devil Heathcliff. It's terrible behaviour, being in the fields after twelve o'clock at night.' *30*

'Silence!' cried Catherine.

'Tell me,' said Hindley, 'were you with Heathcliff last night? Speak the truth, now. You needn't be afraid of harming him. Though I hate him as much as ever, he did me a good deed a short time ago.' *35*

'I never saw Heathcliff last night,' answered Catherine, beginning to cry bitterly. 'If you do send him away from here, I'll go with him. But perhaps you'll never have an opportunity now.' And she burst into terrible sobs.

5 Hindley swore at her and told her to go to her room immediately. I told her to obey, and I shall never forget what happened in her room. I thought she was going mad, and I told Joseph to hurry and fetch the doctor. Dr Kenneth, as soon as he saw her, said she was dangerously ill. She had a
10 very high fever. The doctor treated her and told me what to give her to eat. He told me to be very careful with her as she might be violent, and want to throw herself down the stairs, or out of the window. Then he left, for he had many things to do in the area, where two or three miles was the normal
15 distance between the houses.

Though I cannot say I was a gentle nurse, Joseph and the master were much worse. Our patient was very difficult, but she lived.

Edgar's parents die

Old Mrs Linton paid us several visits, and gave orders to
20 everyone, and in fact made things a lot better. When Catherine was finally getting better, Mrs Linton insisted on taking her to Thrushcross Grange. We were grateful for the peace that this move gave us. But the poor woman had reason to regret her kindness. Both she and her husband caught the fever, and
25 died within a few days of each other.

Our young lady returned to us the same as ever, still very proud and disliking to be put in the wrong. Heathcliff had not been heard of since the evening of the thunder-storm. One day, when Cathy really made me angry, I blamed her for
30 his disappearance. She knew it was true. From that moment, for several months, she only talked to me when she wanted to give me orders, as a servant.

She would not speak to Joseph either, because he always said exactly what he thought. He lectured her as if she were a
35 little girl still, but she thought of herself as a woman, and our

mistress. She thought that her recent illness gave her the right
to behave as she wanted. But if she made anyone angry, she
would cry and say that she was still weak and must not be
scolded.

She stayed away from Mr Earnshaw too, and his compan-   5
ions. Dr Kenneth had told her brother that she could be ill
again if she became too excited. So he allowed her to do whatever she wanted, but he did not think how this might affect
us poor servants.

In fact, Mr Earnshaw was hoping to see her bring honour   10
to the family by a marriage with Edgar Linton. As long as this
appeared to be possible he would let her do as she wished. She
treated us like slaves!

6 Catherine Marries Edgar

Edgar Linton was in love, and he believed himself to be the happiest man in the world on the day he led Catherine to Gimmerton Church for the wedding, three years after his father's death.

5   Although I was unwilling, I was persuaded to leave Wuthering Heights and go with her to her new home. Little Hareton was nearly five years old, and I had just begun to teach him to read. We parted very sadly, but as usual, Catherine got what she wanted, and I had to go. At first I had
10 refused, but Hindley had ordered me out of the house. He wanted no women in the house, he said, now that there was no mistress. The priest would teach Hareton. I had no choice, I had to go.

At Thrushcross Grange, Catherine behaved much better
15 than I had expected. She seemed almost too fond of Mr Linton, and his sister Isabella. They both tried to look after her all the time. I noticed that Mr Edgar was terrified of her bad temper. He did not tell her this, but I saw that if he heard me answer her sharply, he would become upset and frown.

A visit from a stranger
20 But the period of happiness ended. On a warm evening in September, I was coming up from the garden with a heavy basket of apples. It was getting dark, and the moon had just appeared over the high wall of the courtyard. I put my basket down on the steps by the kitchen door, and stood there,
25 enjoying the soft sweet air. My eyes were on the moon, when I heard a voice behind me say:

'Nelly, is that you?'

It was a deep voice, from a stranger, but it sounded famil-iar. I turned, and saw a tall man in dark clothes, with dark
30 skin and hair.

'I have waited here for an hour,' he said. 'And everything around here has been as still as death. I didn't dare enter. Don't you know me? Look, I'm not a stranger.'

I remembered the unforgettable eyes, set deep in his face.

'What?' I cried, as I realised who he was. 'Is it really you Heathcliff?'

'Yes,' he replied, glancing up at the windows, which showed no lights from inside. 'Are they at home? Where is she, Nelly? Nelly, don't look so worried. Is she here? Speak! I must speak to her. Tell her that someone from Gimmerton wishes to see her.'

'How will she take it?' I exclaimed. 'What will she do? You are Heathcliff, but so changed! Where have you been?'

'Go and take my message,' he interrupted me impatiently. 'I must see her!'

When I got to the room where Mr and Mrs Linton were sitting, I could hardly make myself go in. I stood outside the door not knowing what to do. Finally I decided to make an excuse to enter. I would ask them if they wanted to have the candles lit, and so I opened the door.

'Heathcliff's come back!'

They were sitting together in a window seat, looking out onto the wild green hills and the valley of Gimmerton. Wuthering Heights rose above it, but our old house could not be seen from the Grange because it was on the other side of the hill. Both the room and the people in it looked lovely and peaceful. I hated to disturb all this with the news that I brought. At last I said, 'A person from Gimmerton wishes to see you, madam.'

'What does he want?' asked Mrs Linton.

'I did not ask him,' I answered.

'Well, close the curtains, Nelly, and bring up tea,' she said. 'I won't be long.'

She left the room. Mr Edgar asked who it was.

'Someone the mistress does not expect,' I replied. 'That Heathcliff, you remember him sir, he used to live at Wuthering Heights.'

'What! The wild boy, the rough, rude one?' he cried. 'Why didn't you tell Catherine that?'

'Hush! You mustn't use those names about him, sir,' I said. 'You'll make the mistress angry. She was very unhappy
5   when he ran away.'

Mr Linton walked to a window on the other side of the room that overlooked the courtyard. He called out, 'Don't stand down there, Cathy! Bring the person in.'

I heard the door close, and Catherine rushed upstairs,
10   breathless and wild, too excited to show happiness.

'O Edgar, Edgar!' she cried, throwing her arms around his neck. 'O Edgar darling! Heathcliff's come back.'

'Well, well,' cried her husband, angrily, 'don't choke me for that. I never thought he was such a wonderful thing. There is
15   no need to be so excited.'

'I know you didn't like him,' she answered. 'But for my sake, you must be friends now. Shall I tell him to come up?'

'Here?'

'Where else?' she asked. He looked troubled, and suggested
20   that the kitchen might be a more suitable place.

'No,' she said, after a while. 'I cannot sit in the kitchen. Bring another table here, Ellen, one for your master and Miss Isabella, being high class, the other for Heathcliff and myself, being of the lower ranks.'

25   She was going to run off again, but Edgar stopped her. He turned to me, and said, 'You ask him to come up. Catherine, try to be glad without being so silly. The servants need not see you welcoming a bad servant like a brother.'

I went downstairs, and found Heathcliff waiting, expecting
30   an invitation to enter. He followed me without saying any-thing, and I took him up to the master and mistress. The lady ran forward, took both his hands, and led him to Linton.

Heathcliff has changed

Now I could see quite clearly by the light of the fire and the candles, and I was amazed to see how much Heathcliff
35   had changed. He had grown tall and straight, a well-formed

man. Beside him, my master seemed quite small and youth-like. His manner of standing and walking suggested that he had probably been in the army. His face looked much older than Mr Linton's, as though he was used to making difficult decisions. He looked intelligent, and showed none of the ef-   5
fects of his former treatment at Wuthering Heights. There was still perhaps a certain wildness behind those eyes, full of black fire, but it was controlled, and his manner was very dignified. There was no roughness left, though his manner was too stern to be charming. My master's surprise was even   10
greater than mine. For a moment, he did not know how to speak to the servant, as he had called him.

'Sit down, sir,' he said, at last. 'Mrs Linton, remembering old times, wants me to welcome you. And of course I am happy when anything happens to please her.'   15

'And I also,' answered Heathcliff, 'especially if it is any-thing in which I have a part.'

He took a seat opposite Catherine, who kept looking at her old friend as though she feared he would disappear if she took her eyes from him. He did not look at her often, a quick   20
glance now and then was enough. Mr Edgar became pale with anger when he realised that his wife was only interested in Heathcliff that evening.

Catherine rose, and laughed like someone who was totally happy. 'I shall think it was all a dream by tomorrow!' she   25
cried. 'I shall not be able to believe that I have seen, and touched, and spoken to you once more. And yet, cruel Heathcliff, you don't deserve this welcome. You were absent and silent for three years, and never thought of me!'

'I thought of you a little more than you have thought of   30
me,' he said quietly. 'I heard of your marriage, Cathy, not long ago. I just wanted to see you once more, afterwards to settle my affairs with Hindley. Then I wanted to take the law into my own hands and kill myself. Your welcome has put these ideas out of my head, but I have had a hard life since I   35
last heard your voice. You must forgive me, for I struggled only for you!'

'Catherine,' said Edgar, 'unless we are to have cold tea, please come to the table. Mr Heathcliff will have a long walk, wherever he is staying tonight, and I'm thirsty.'

Heathcliff is staying at Wuthering Heights

Their guest did not stay much longer than an hour. I asked,
5 as he left, if he was staying in Gimmerton.

'No, Wuthering Heights,' he answered. 'Mr Earnshaw invited me when I called this morning.'

Mr Earnshaw invited him! And *he* visited Mr Earnshaw. I didn't understand this at all. I had a feeling in the bottom of
10 my heart that it would have been better for everyone if he had stayed away from this place forever.

In the middle of the night I was woken up by Mrs Linton coming into my room. She took a seat by my bed, and pulled me by the hair to prevent me sleeping.

15 'I cannot rest, Ellen,' she said, 'and I want someone to keep me company in my happiness. Edgar is angry because I'm glad about a thing that does not interest him. He said I was cruel to talk when he was so sick and sleepy. I said a few nice things about Heathcliff, and he, either because he had a
20 headache or because he was jealous, would not listen and told me to be quiet.'

'What use is it praising Heathcliff to him?' I answered. 'As boys they hated each other, and Heathcliff would dislike it just as much to hear you praising Mr Linton. It's human
25 nature. Don't talk to Mr Linton about him.'

'But it shows great weakness, doesn't it, Nelly? I'm not jealous,' she answered.

'What do you think about Heathcliff going to Wuthering Heights?' I asked. 'He has changed in every way, it seems. He
30 is quite a Christian, offering to be friends with all his old enemies!'

'He explained it,' she replied. 'I wondered about it as much as you. He said he called at Wuthering Heights to get information about me from you, thinking that you still lived there.
35 Joseph told Hindley, who came out and, after some questioning, asked Heathcliff to go inside. There were some people

sitting playing cards. Heathcliff joined them. My brother lost
some money to him and, finding that Heathcliff seemed to
have a lot of money, asked him if he would like to come
again in the evening. Hindley is not very careful in making
his friends. He doesn't worry about trusting someone like   5
Heathcliff, whom he has treated so badly. But Heathcliff says
that his main reason for staying there is because it is close to
the Grange.'

'It's a terrible place for a young man to choose to stay in!'
I exclaimed. 'Have you no fear for what might happen, Mrs   10
Linton?'

'None for my friend. His strong head will keep him from
danger. I am more afraid for Hindley. But he can't be made
much worse than he is already, and, with my power over
Heathcliff, no physical harm will come to my brother.'   15

Isabella falls in love with Heathcliff

Heathcliff, or Mr Heathcliff as we called him now, did not
come to Thrushcross Grange too often at first. He seemed to
be estimating how his visits affected Mr Linton. Catherine,
also, was quite careful about expressing her pleasure in seeing
him, and he gradually began to visit regularly. Mr Linton's   20
earlier suspicion was quietened as Mr Heathcliff's behaviour
was perfectly correct at all times.

Then Mr Linton had a new reason to worry. His sister,
Isabella appeared to have fallen in love with the new Heathcliff. She was then a charming young lady of eighteen, still   25
young in many ways. But she was intelligent, and had a difficult temper if made angry. Her brother, who loved her dearly,
was both amazed and worried by what had happened to his
sister. He did not want her to marry someone who had no
real name. Furthermore, if Linton himself had no son, his   30
property would then go to Heathcliff. He had sensed Heathcliff's true character, and he knew that, although Heathcliff
looked different on the outside, his mind could never be
changed. And he feared Heathcliff's mind. He was terrified of
the idea of Isabella being ruled by it. He would have been even   35

more worried and upset if he had known that Isabella's feelings were not returned. As soon as he discovered his sister's feelings, he had blamed Heathcliff for deliberately encouraging her.

5   We had all noticed that Miss Linton was upset over something. She became angry and unpleasant, but we excused her because we thought she was ill. Catherine insisted that she should go to bed and said she would send for the doctor. Mention of Dr Kenneth caused Isabella to exclaim immediate-
10   ly that her health was perfect, and it was only Catherine's cruelty which made her unhappy.

'How can you say I am cruel?' cried the mistress, amazed. 'When have I been cruel, tell me?'

'Yesterday,' sobbed Isabella, 'and now!'

15   'Yesterday, when?'

'In our walk along the moor. You told me to go where I liked, while you walked with Mr Heathcliff.'

'And that's your idea of cruelty?' said Catherine, laughing. 'It wasn't because we didn't want you there. I only thought
20   that you might have found our conversation boring.'

'Oh no,' wept the young lady, 'you wanted me to go away because you knew I wanted to be there!'

'What is she talking about?' asked Mrs Linton, turning to me.

25   'I wanted to be with him, and I won't always be sent off,' continued Isabella, getting angry. 'You want no one to be loved except yourself!'

'You are a stupid little monkey!' said Mrs Linton, in surprise. 'It is impossible that you can feel like this towards
30   Heathcliff, or even find him a pleasant person.'

'It is not,' said the girl. 'I love him more than you have ever loved Edgar. And he might love me, if you would let him.'

'I wouldn't like to be you!' Catherine declared, and she
35   seemed to speak sincerely. 'Nelly, help me to show her how mad this is. Tell her what Heathcliff is, a wild creature, dangerous and uncontrollable. You do not know his character,

child, or else you would not have dreams like these. Please
don't think that he hides a kind nature underneath a stern
appearance. He's a fierce, cruel man. He'd crush you like an
egg, Isabella, if he found you troublesome. He could never
love a Linton. But he'd be quite capable of marrying your   5
fortune. There's my picture of him, and I'm his friend.'

Miss Linton looked at her sister-in-law with horror.

'For shame!' she cried. 'You are worse than twenty
enemies, you poisonous friend!'

'You think I speak from wicked selfishness?' said Catherine.   10
'Good! Try for yourself, if that's what you think.'

Isabella sobbed as Mrs Linton left the room. 'All is against
me,' she cried. 'But she wasn't telling the truth, was she? Mr
Heathcliff is not a devil. He has a good soul, and a true one,
or how could he remember her?'   15

'Don't think of him any more, Miss,' I said. 'He's a bad
person, no husband for you. Mrs Linton spoke strongly, and
yet I cannot disagree. And she knows him better than anyone
else and she would never pretend he was worse than he is. Besides, honest people don't hide what they've done. How has   20
he been living? How has he got rich? Why is he staying at
Wuthering Heights, in the house of a man that he hates? Mr
Earnshaw has become worse and worse since he went to live
there. They sit up all night together, and Hindley has been
borrowing money on his land, and does nothing but play   25
cards and drink. Joseph told me this, I met him in Gimmerton.
No, Joseph may be a horrible old man, but he doesn't lie.'

'You are just like the rest, Nelly!' she replied. 'I won't
listen to your horrid stories any more.'

The next day, Mr Edgar had to go to a meeting in the next   30
town. Mr Heathcliff, knowing that the master was going to be
out, called rather earlier than usual. Catherine and Isabella
were sitting together in the library. They were silent, and
each looked angry with the other.

Catherine tells Heathcliff about Isabella's feelings

Catherine rose and laughed when she saw Mr Heathcliff   35

pass the window. Isabella, taking no notice of Catherine, did not realize what was happening. By the time the door opened and Mr Heathcliff was shown in, it was too late to try to escape.

5 'Come in,' cried the mistress, 'here are two people sadly in need of a third. Heathcliff, I'm proud to show you, at last, somebody who likes you more than I do myself. No, it's not Nelly. Don't look at her! My poor little sister-in-law is break- ing her heart for you. You could become Edgar's brother. No,
10 Isabella, you shan't run off,' she continued, holding on to the confused girl, who had been about to run from the room.

'Mr Heathcliff,' said Isabella, 'be kind enough to tell this friend of yours to let me go. She forgets that you and I are not close friends, and what amuses her is extremely painful
15 to me.'

The guest did not answer, but took his seat. He looked as though he didn't care how she felt towards him, and she turned and whispered to Catherine to let her go.

'No, I won't,' Mrs Linton answered. 'You shall stay. Now
20 then, Heathcliff, why don't you look more pleased with my pleasant news? Isabella swears that the love I have for Edgar is nothing to that which she has for you.'

'I think that you are wrong,' said Heathcliff. 'She wishes to be out of here now, anyway.'

25 He stared hard at Isabella, as one might do at a strange, ugly animal. The poor girl couldn't bear that. She grew white and red in quick succession. With tears in her eyes, she bent to loosen the firm grasp of Catherine's hand. As she could not remove Catherine's fingers, she began to make use of her
30 nails.

'There's a cat for you!' exclaimed Mrs Linton, setting her free, and shaking her hand with pain. 'Go away, for God's sake, and hide yourself. How foolish to show those nails to him! What do you think he'll think? Look, Heathcliff, they
35 are dangerous instruments, you must be careful of your eyes.'

'I'd pull them off her fingers if they ever did me any harm,' he answered cruelly, when the door had closed after her. 'But

what did you mean by making fun of her like that, Cathy?
You were not speaking the truth, were you?'

'I certainly was,' she replied. 'She has been in love with
you for several weeks now, and she has been in a temper with
me because I told her what a bad character you have. But
don't worry about it any more.'

'I don't like her at all,' he said. 'You'd hear of odd things
if I lived alone with that pale face. Her eyes are just like
Linton's, horrible!'

'They at least are lovely,' said Catherine. 'They are angel's
eyes!'

'She gets all her brother's property at his death, doesn't
she?'

'There are a number of nephews as well, but let's talk of
something else.'

'But,' said Heathcliff, 'though Isabella Linton may be silly,
she is not mad. However, we'll forget the matter, as you say.'

They stopped talking about it, and Catherine, probably,
stopped thinking about it. Heathcliff, I felt certain, remembered it often during the evening. I saw him smile to himself.
He looked wicked, and I felt sure he was planning something.

I determined to watch his movements. I usually took the
master's side rather than Catherine's, because he was kind and
trusting and honourable. She was not exactly dishonest, but
I had little faith in her principles, and still less sympathy for
her feelings. I wanted something to happen which might free
both Wuthering Heights and the Grange from Mr Heathcliff's
influence, leaving us as we had been, before he had come
back. His visits were like a bad dream to me, and, I suspected,
to my master as well. I hated him living at Wuthering Heights
but I could not explain why. I felt that an evil beast was
walking between the Heights and the Grange, waiting for
the right time to jump upon us and destroy us.

7 A Terrible Quarrel between Heathcliff and Edgar

Sometimes while I was thinking of these things by myself, I've got up in sudden terror, and put on my hat to go and see how everything was at Wuthering Heights. I've persuaded myself that it was my duty to warn Mr Hindley how people
5 were talking about him and his bad ways. But then I've remembered his determination to be wicked, and I've been too afraid to go back to that dark, unfriendly house.

Once I passed the old gate, going out of my way, on a journey to Gimmerton. I felt a deep desire to be at the
10 Heights. The nearer I got to the house the more worried I grew. When I saw it, I trembled all over. There was a figure standing near the gate, and looking out through it.

Ellen sees Hareton again

That was my first idea, when I saw a brown-eyed boy with his face pressed against the bars. Then, when I was able to
15 think a little more calmly, I realized that this must be Hareton, my Hareton. He was not greatly changed since I had left him ten months before.

'God bless you, darling!' I cried, forgetting at once my foolish fears. 'Hareton, it's Nelly – Nelly, your nurse.'
20 He backed away, out of my reach, and picked up a stone.

'I have come to see your father, Hareton,' I added. I guessed from the way he behaved that Nelly, if he remembered her at all, was not recognised as me.

He raised his hand to throw the stone. I started to speak
25 to him, to calm him, but it did no good. The stone struck my hat. Then the child started to swear at me, shouting horrible words that are not fit to be heard from anyone, especially a child! Almost ready to cry, I took an orange from my pocket, and offered it to him. I hoped in this way to make friends
30 with him. He hesitated, and then grabbed it from me. I showed him another, keeping it out of his reach.

'Who has taught you those terrible words?' I asked, 'The priest?'

'The priest is stupid, and you too! Give me that!' he replied.

5   'Who's your master, then? Tell me and you shall have it.'

'Devil Daddy,' was his answer.

'And what do you learn from Daddy?' I continued.

'Nothing, but to keep out of his way. Daddy doesn't like me because I swear at him.'

10 'And the devil teaches you to swear at Daddy?'

'No, Heathcliff.'

I asked if he liked Mr Heathcliff. 'Yes,' he answered. 'He treats my father the way my father treats me. He swears at Daddy for swearing at me. He says I may do as I please.'

15 'And the priest does not teach you to read and write any more?'

'No,' I was told, 'the priest should have his teeth pushed down his throat if he dared to come near Wuthering Heights. Heathcliff promised that!'

20 I put the orange into his hand, and told him to tell his father that Nelly Dean was waiting to speak to him. He went in, but instead of Hindley coming out, it was Heathcliff who appeared at the doorstep. I turned away and ran down the road as fast as I could. Something terrified me about that

25 black figure standing there in the doorway of Wuthering Heights.

Heathcliff and Isabella

The next time Heathcliff came to the Grange, Miss Isabella happened to be in the garden feeding the birds. She hadn't spoken to her sister-in-law for three days, but she had stopped

30 her dreadful complaining. We all found it much more peaceful. Heathcliff had never taken any trouble to be nice to Miss Linton, I knew. Now, as soon as he appeared in the garden and saw her, he took a quick look around to make sure that there was no one else there. I was standing in the kitchen, by

35 the window, but I drew back so that he could not see me. Then he stepped over to Miss Isabella, and said something.

She seemed upset and looked as though she wanted to leave him, but he laid his hand on her arm. There was another rapid look at the house; and thinking himself unseen, the devil took her in his arms and kissed her.

'Wicked!' I exclaimed. 'You are a liar and a cheat too, are you?'   *5*

'Who is it, Nelly?' said Catherine's voice at my elbow. I had not noticed her come in.

'Your worthless friend!' I said angrily. 'Ah, he has seen us, he is coming in! I wonder if he will have a good excuse for   *10* kissing Miss Isabella, when he told you he hated her.'

Mrs Linton saw Isabella pull herself free, and run out of the garden. A minute later Heathcliff was opening the door and coming inside. Catherine angrily ordered me to be quiet.

'To hear you, people might think that you were the   *15* mistress,' she said. 'Heathcliff, what have you been doing, causing this trouble? I said you must leave Isabella alone. Please do, unless you want Edgar to forbid you to come here any more.'

'Let's hope that he does not try!' answered the devil. 'Let   *20* God help him to keep his temper! Every day I want to send him to heaven more and more!'

'Hush,' said Catherine. 'Don't make me angry. Did she come across to you on purpose?'

'What does it matter to you?' he muttered. 'I have a right   *25* to kiss her if she wants me to. You have no right to object. I am not your husband. You needn't be jealous of me.'

'I'm not jealous of you,' replied the mistress. 'I am worried about you. If you like Isabella, you shall marry her. But do you really like her? Tell the truth, Heathcliff. There, you   *30* won't answer. I'm certain you don't.'

'And would Mr Linton approve of his sister marrying that man?' I asked.

'Mr Linton would approve,' replied the mistress with determination.   *35*

'He needn't bother to worry about it,' said Heathcliff. 'I don't need his approval. And as for you Catherine, I have a few things to say to you while we're here. I want you to

realise that I know you have treated me badly, really badly! Do you hear? And if you think that I don't know it, you are a fool. And if you think that you can make me happy again with a few soft words you are even more of a fool. And if
5   you think that I'll suffer without revenge, I'll convince you otherwise in a very short time. Meanwhile, thank you for telling me your sister-in-law's secret. I swear I'll make the most of it. Even if it means going against your wishes!'

'I've treated you badly?' repeated Catherine in amazement.
10 'And you'll take your revenge? You appear determined to create a quarrel. Quarrel with Edgar, if you please, Heathcliff, and deceive his sister. You've hit on the most effective method of revenging yourself on me.'

'I want no revenge on you,' replied Heathcliff less strongly,
15 and the conversation ended.

Edgar Linton is angry

Mrs Linton sat down by the fire, upset and angry. Heathcliff stood next to her with folded arms, thinking his evil thoughts. In this position I left them to look for the master, who was wondering what kept Cathy below in the kitchen so
20 long.

'Ellen,' he said, when I entered, 'have you seen your mistress?'

'Yes, she's in the kitchen, sir,' I answered. 'She's very upset by Mr Heathcliff's behaviour. Indeed, I do think it's time to
25 arrange his visits rather differently. It's harmful to be too soft, and now this has happened.' And I told him of what happened in the garden, and the talk that followed afterwards with Catherine. Edgar Linton had difficulty in letting me finish. His first words showed that he was not sure that his
30 wife was free from blame.

'This is unbearable!' he exclaimed. 'It is disgraceful that she should have him for a friend, and force his company on me! Call two men from the yard for me, Ellen. Catherine shall not argue with this terrible man any longer. I have per-
35 mitted it long enough.'

He went downstairs, and telling the servants to wait in the hall, he went into the kitchen. I followed him. Catherine and Heathcliff had continued their angry discussion. Mrs Linton was scolding with even more energy than before. Heathcliff had moved to the window, and bowed his head, as though 5 her anger had had some effect.

He saw the master first, and made a hurried sign to her to be quiet. She obeyed, when she saw why.

'What is this?' said Linton, speaking to her. 'How can you stay here, after this animal has spoken to you like that? I 10 suppose you are used to this sort of behaviour from him. Perhaps you imagine that I can get used to it too!'

'Have you been listening at the door, Edgar?' asked the mistress, in a voice that always made her husband angry. The tone of her voice was indeed most unpleasant. 15

Heathcliff, who had raised his eyes on hearing Catherine speak like that, laughed unpleasantly at Mr Linton, on purpose it seemed, to draw Mr Linton's attention to him.

He succeeded, but Edgar did not mean to entertain him with long speeches. 20

'I have permitted you to come here up to now, sir,' he said quietly, 'because I felt you were only partly responsible for your miserable character. I knew that Catherine wished to continue seeing you, and so I agreed, foolishly. But your presence here is poisonous. Because of this, and to prevent 25 worse things happening, I forbid you to come to this house ever again. I tell you now that I wish you to leave immediately.'

Heathcliff looked at the size of the speaker, with scorn in his eyes. 30

'Cathy, this lamb of yours threatens like a bull!' he said. 'It is in danger of coming to some harm against my fists. By God, Mr Linton, I am only sorry that you are not worth knocking down!'

My master gave a quick look towards the hall, and signalled 35 to me to get the men. He had no intention of fighting Heathcliff himself.

I obeyed the hint, but Mrs Linton, suspecting something, followed. When I tried to call them, she pulled me back, banged the door shut, and locked it.

'Fight fair!' she said, in answer to her husband's look of
5 angry surprise. 'If you do not have the courage to fight him, say you are sorry, or allow yourself to be beaten. It will teach you not to pretend to be braver than you really are. No, I'll swallow the key before you shall get it! So this is how I am rewarded for my kindness to both of you. Edgar, I was
10 defending you and your property. I hope Heathcliff beats you until you are sick for daring to think an evil thought of me!'

It did not need a beating to produce that effect on the master. He tried to get the key from Catherine by force, so
15 for safety she threw it into the hottest part of the fire. When she did this Mr Edgar began to shake all over, and his face went deathly pale. He couldn't stop himself. He was so upset that he leant on the back of a chair and covered his face with his hands.

20 'Oh, heavens!' exclaimed Mrs Linton. 'Heathcliff will not lift a finger against you. Cheer up! You won't be hurt! You are weaker than a lamb, even, more like a hare!'

'I wish you joy of the coward, Cathy!' said her friend. 'And this is the weak thing that you preferred to me! I would
25 not hit him with my fist, but I'd kick him with my foot. Is he weeping, or is he going to faint with fear?'

Edgar attacks Heathcliff

Heathcliff approached and gave the chair, on which Linton rested, a push. He'd have done better to have kept his distance. My master jumped up, and hit him full on the throat
30 a blow that would have caused a smaller man to fall. It took Heathcliff's breath away for a minute, and while he was recovering, Mr Linton walked out by the back door into the courtyard, and from there to the front entrance.

'There! Now you can't come here any more,' cried
35 Catherine. 'Get away now. He'll return with guns and more

men. He'll never forgive you. You've done me a bad deed, Heathcliff. But go – hurry! I'd rather see Edgar caught, fighting for his life, than you!'

'Do you think I'm going, with a blow like that burning in my throat?' he shouted. 'No! I'll break his bones like rotten   *5* nuts before I leave this place! If I don't do it now, I shall murder him later. So, if you want him to live, you had better let me hit him now!'

'He's not coming,' I interrupted, telling a small lie. 'There are three servants coming instead. Surely you don't want to   *10* wait to be forced out of the house by them? The master will probably be watching from an upstairs window.'

The servants were there, but Linton was with them. They had already entered the courtyard. Heathcliff, on second thoughts, decided to avoid a struggle against three servants.   *15* He seized a stick, broke the lock on the inner door, and made his escape as the others came in.

Mrs Linton, who was very excited by all this, told me to take her upstairs. She did not know my share in the disturbance, and I was anxious to keep it from her.   *20*

'I don't know what to do, Nelly,' she exclaimed, throwing herself on the sofa. 'Make sure that Isabella knows that I don't want to see her. All this started because of her. If anyone makes me angry now, I shall go mad! And Nelly, say to Edgar, if you see him again tonight, that I am in danger of   *25* being seriously ill. I hope it comes true. He has upset me so much. I want to frighten him. Why did he come and listen to our argument? Heathcliff's talk was terrible after you left us, but I could soon have taken his thoughts away from Isabella. Now nothing can be done! If Edgar had never heard our   *30* conversation, he would never have suffered. Really, when he started his conversation by questioning me in that tone of voice, after I had been fighting Heathcliff for him, I hardly cared what they did to each other. Especially as I realized that, however it ended, we would all be driven apart for a   *35* long time. Well, if I cannot keep Heathcliff for my friend, if Edgar will be mean and jealous, I'll try to break their hearts by breaking my own. That will be a quick way of finishing it all.' She looked up at me as she finished speaking, and said with some anger, 'I wish *you* could look a little more anxious about me!'

Catherine quarrels with Edgar

5   I did not wish to frighten her husband, or to increase his anger in order to satisfy her selfishness, so I said nothing when I met the master coming towards the sitting room. But I stopped to listen, to see whether they would take up their quarrel again.

10   He began to speak first.

'Remain where you are, Catherine,' he said, with sadness rather than anger in his voice. 'I shall not stay, but I must learn, after this evening's events, whether you mean to continue your friendship with — '

15   'Oh, for heaven's sake,' interrupted the mistress, stamping her foot, 'for heaven's sake, let's not hear any more about that now! Your cold blood cannot be made hot. Your veins may be full of iced water, but mine are boiling, and the sight of such cold calmness makes me angry.'

20   'If you want me to go you must answer my question, then I'll leave,' said Mr Linton. 'You must answer it, and your violence does not frighten me. I know that you can be as calm as you like, when you please. Will you give up Heathcliff from now on, or will you give me up? It is impossible for you

25 to be my friend and his at the same time. I insist on having an answer now.'

'And I insist that you leave me alone!' exclaimed Catherine angrily. 'I demand it! Don't you see I can hardly stand? Edgar, leave me!'

30   She rang the bell till it broke with a snap, but I entered slowly. Her rages were so senseless and stupid. There she lay, beating her head against the arm of the sofa. Mr Linton stood looking at her in sudden sympathy and fear. He told me to fetch some water.

35   I brought a full glass, and, because she would not drink, I

sprinkled it on her face. In a few seconds she stretched herself out stiff, and turned up her eyes, while her cheeks went white and grey. She looked like death. Linton was terrified.

'There is nothing wrong,' I whispered. I did not want him to give in, although I could not help being afraid in my heart.   5

'She has blood on her lips!' he said, trembling.

'Never mind!' I answered. And I told him how she had decided, before he came in, to behave like this.

Unfortunately I said this aloud, and she heard me, for she jumped up, her eyes flashing. I decided I would get broken   10
bones, at the very least, but she didn't come towards me. She looked around her quickly, and then rushed from the room. The master told me to follow her, which I did, but she had locked herself in her bedroom, away from us all.

Catherine refuses to eat

Next morning she did not come down to breakfast, so I   15
went to ask her if she would like me to bring her some food.

'No!' she replied, and would say nothing else.

The same question was repeated outside her door at dinner, and tea, and again, on the next day, but the same answer was received.   20

Mr Linton spent his time in the library, and did not ask what his wife was doing. Isabella and he had talked for an hour. He had tried to persuade her of the badness of Heathcliff's character and to make her realize the horror of accepting his friendship. But he did not understand her replies,   25
whether she would or would not encourage Heathcliff. So their talk ended very unsatisfactorily. However, he did warn her that if she did encourage Heathcliff he would no longer consider her his sister.

8 Isabella and Heathcliff

Miss Linton wandered about the fields and garden, always silent, and almost always in tears. Her brother shut himself up among his books that he never opened, and Catherine refused to eat. Each, I think, was waiting for the other to
5 come and say they were sorry. They were waiting for someone's pride to weaken. I went about my household duties, convinced that the Grange had only one sensible soul in its walls, and that was inside my body.

On the third day, Mrs Linton unlocked her door. She had
10 finished her water that always stood in her room in a jug, and she wanted some more, as well as some soup. She believed she was dying. I decided she had only told me that in order to worry Edgar. I believed she was telling a lie so I kept it to myself, and brought her some tea and dry toast. She ate and
15 drank eagerly, and then sank back on her pillows again, groaning.

'Oh, I will die,' she exclaimed, 'since no one cares anything about me. I wish I had not eaten that.'

Then, a little while later I heard her mutter, 'No, I'll not
20 die. He'd be glad. He does not love me at all, he would never miss me!'

'Do you want anything, madam?' I asked, getting rather worried now. Her fever seemed to be quite real. She began tossing about and tearing at the pillow with her teeth. She
25 started tearing out the feathers in great handfuls. Then she raised herself and asked me to open the window. We were in the middle of winter, and I refused.

Terrible dreams

The changes in her moods were beginning to alarm me terribly. Before she had been violent, now she was returning
30 to her childhood, calling out the names of birds that she and Heathcliff had seen on the moor.

She was silent for a time, then she seized me suddenly.

'Oh dear! I thought I was at home at Wuthering Heights again,' she sighed. 'I thought I was lying in my room there. Because I'm weak my brain got confused. Don't say anything, but stay with me. I am afraid of sleeping alone. My dreams   5
terrify me.'

'A deep sleep would do you good, madam,' I answered.

'Oh, if only I were in my own bed in the old house!' she cried. 'With that wind sounding in the fir trees! Do let me have one breath!'   10

To quieten her, I held the window open for a few seconds. A cold wind rushed through. I closed it and returned to her side. She lay still now, her face covered in tears. Her body was tired and her spirit beaten. Our fierce Catherine had become a weeping child!   15

'How long have I been shut in here?' she asked.

'You locked yourself in on Monday evening,' I replied, 'and this is Thursday night, or rather Friday morning, at present.'

'What? Of the same week? Only that short time?'   20

'Long enough to live on cold water and bad temper,' I said.

'Well, it seemed such a long time,' she muttered doubtfully. 'It must be more. I remember being in the sitting room after Heathcliff had left, then Edgar coming in and making me so angry, and me running into this room, quite desperate. As   25
soon as I had locked this door, complete blackness came over me, and I fell on the floor. When I began to recover, to be able to see and hear, it was already dawn. Nelly, I'll tell you what I thought as I lay there. I thought I was in my bed at home, and my heart was nearly breaking with some kind of   30
sorrow. I thought I was a child, my father had just been buried, and my misery had come from the separation that Hindley had ordered between me and Heathcliff.

'Oh, I'm burning! I wish I were outside! I wish I were a girl again, half wild and strong and free, and laughing at injuries.   35
Why am I so changed? Why do I feel so feverish at a few angry words? I'm sure I would feel better if I could go up

there on the moors. Open the window again, wide – keep it open! Quick! Why don't you move?'

'Because I won't let you die of cold,' I answered.

'You won't give me a chance of life, you mean. However,
5   I'm not helpless yet. I'll open it myself.'

Getting up from the bed before I could stop her, she crossed the room, walking unsteadily. She threw open the window, and leant out, taking no notice of the icy wind that must have cut into her bare shoulders like a knife. My words
10 had no effect on her so at last I tried to get her away from the window by force. But in her fever, her strength was much greater than mine.

Outside there was no moon, and everything below lay in darkness. No light showed from any house, far or near. Those
15 at Wuthering Heights had never been visible from the Grange, yet Catherine insisted that night that she could see them shining.

'Look! That's my room with the candle in it, and the trees swaying in front of it. That other candle is from Joseph's
20 room. He's waiting for me to come home, so that he can lock the gate after me. He'll have to wait a bit longer yet. It's a rough journey, and we must pass by Gimmerton Church on that journey. We've often been in the churchyard together at night, and dared the ghosts to come out. Heathcliff, if I ask
25 you now, will you come? If you do, I'll keep you. I'll not lie there by myself. They may bury me twelve feet deep, but I won't rest until you are with me. I never will!'

Edgar discovers Catherine's illness

Then to my alarm, I heard the door opening, and Mr Linton entered. He had heard our talking and had been
30 attracted by curiosity, or fear, to find out why we were still up at that late hour.

'Oh sir!' I cried. 'My poor mistress is ill, and I cannot make her go to bed at all. Please come and help, and persuade her yourself. Forget your anger, for she needs help desperately.'
35 'Catherine ill?' he said, coming towards us quickly. 'Shut the window, Ellen. Catherine – '

He fell silent. The sight of Mrs Linton's appearance made him speechless, and he could only look from her to me in horrified astonishment.

'She's been in here,' I continued, 'refusing to eat or say anything. She wouldn't let any of us come in till this evening, so we couldn't tell you that she was ill. We didn't know it ourselves, but it's nothing.'

I felt I had explained badly. The master frowned.

'It is nothing, is it? You will have to explain yourself more clearly than this. Why didn't you tell me before?' He took his wife in his arms, but at first she didn't seem to recognize him at all. Then she realized who it was that held her.

'Ah! You have come, have you, Edgar Linton?' she said, angrily. 'You are one of those things that are always found when never wanted, and when you are wanted, never! I suppose you are going to argue with me and scold me now, I can see you are. But you cannot keep me from my narrow home out there in the churchyard, my resting place. That is where I shall be going before spring is ended! Not among the Lintons, don't forget, not under the church roof, but in the open air with a stone to mark my grave.'

'Catherine, what is the matter?' cried the master. 'Don't I mean anything to you any more? Do you love that man Heathcliff?'

'Hush!' cried Mrs Linton, 'hush, this moment! If you mention that name again, I'll end the matter immediately, by jumping from the window. I don't want you, Edgar. Not any more. Return to your books. I'm glad you have something to turn to, for all that you had in me is gone.'

'Her mind is wandering, sir,' I said. 'She has been talking nonsense all evening. When she quietens and the doctor comes to care for her, everything will be all right. But from now on, we must be careful not to make her angry again.'

'I do not want any more advice from you,' answered Mr Linton. 'You knew she should not be made angry, yet you encouraged me to annoy her. And you never even gave me a hint of how she has been these last three days. You have been

cruel and thoughtless. Months of sickness could not have
caused such a change!'

I began to defend myself, but Mr Linton stopped me. He
did not want to be reminded of the quarrel with Heathcliff.
5 But at the mention of Heathcliff's name, Catherine, confused
as she was, realized what had happened when I had left the
kitchen three days before.

'Ah! It was Nelly then, who is my secret enemy! Let me
go, and I'll make her sorry!'

10 She struggled desperately to get free from Mr Linton's
arms. I decided it was better not to stay, and left the room,
determined to get a doctor as soon as possible, even if Mr
Linton had not yet told me to.

The doctor comes

It was two o'clock in the morning when I reached Dr
15 Kenneth's house in the village. He had just come back from
another house, where a woman had been having trouble with
a baby. My account of Catherine Linton's illness persuaded
him to come back with me immediately to Thrushcross
Grange. He was a plain, rough man, and he spoke plainly. He
20 said that he doubted if she could survive another attack like
the one before, unless she proved to be a better patient and
followed his instructions.

'Nelly Dean,' he said, 'I can't help thinking that something
terrible must have happened, to make this illness of Catherine's
25 return. What has been happening at the Grange? We've heard
some odd things here. A strong girl like Catherine does not
fall ill over nothing. How did it happen?'

'The master will inform you,' I answered, 'but you know
how violent the Earnshaws are. But I will say this, it started
30 with a quarrel. Then she collapsed. That's her story, at least,
for she rushed out of the room in the middle of the quarrel,
and locked herself up in her room. Afterwards she refused to
eat, and now she remains in a half dream. She knows those
around her, but her mind is full of all sorts of strange ideas
35 and imaginary things.'

'Haven't Mr Linton and Mr Heathcliff been quite friendly recently?'

'Heathcliff frequently visits the Grange,' I answered. 'Because he and the mistress were friends as children, rather than because the master wants to see him. Now, he's been told not to call any more, because he has shown more than a friendly interest in Miss Linton. I doubt that he will be allowed near the place again.'

Isabella has gone

'Isabella is a real little fool. I have already been told that last night she and Heathcliff were walking in the woods at the back of your house for about two hours. He was trying to persuade her to mount his horse and ride away with him. The person who told me this said that Miss Isabella promised to be ready to do the same thing on their meeting after that. You had better tell Mr Linton about it all so that he can make plans to prevent any such thing happening!'

This news filled me with fresh fears. When we got back I left the doctor with Mrs Linton and rushed upstairs to Miss Isabella's room. There was no one in the room, it was empty. If only she had known of Mrs Linton's illness, they wouldn't have gone. But now what could be done? I could not follow them, and I dared not tell the family, and fill the place with more confusion. My master had already enough to think about with Catherine's illness, and had no time to spare for any more sorrow and worry. So, I could see no better thing to do than to say nothing at all, and hold my tongue.

Catherine lay on her bed in a troubled sleep. Her husband had succeeded in calming her. The doctor examined her and spoke hopefully to him of the illness ending happily, if only we could make sure that she was never upset, but always peaceful and calm. He told me when we were alone that he did not think that the real danger was death, but rather that her brain might be damaged permanently.

I did not close my eyes that night, nor did Mr Linton. Indeed we didn't even go to bed. The servants were all up, long before their normal hour, moving through the house quietly, and exchanging whispers. Everyone was active except Miss Isabella, and they began to say how long she slept. Her brother, too, asked if she had woken up. He seemed to want her near him, and it hurt him that she was showing no anxiety 5 about her sister-in-law.

I was afraid that he would send me to call her, but I was not the first to tell him of her escape. One of the maids, who had been to the village of Gimmerton that morning, came rushing into the room.

10 'Oh! Master, master! Our young lady, she's gone!' cried the girl.

'What's the matter?' cried Mr Linton, 'What did you say has happened to your young lady?'

'Miss Isabella's gone,' the girl repeated. 'I met the lad, that 15 brings the milk here, on my way to Gimmerton. He said a lady and gentleman had stopped to have a horse's shoe fastened two miles out of Gimmerton, not long after midnight last night. They were seen by the workman's daughter, and she knew who they were immediately. Heathcliff and 20 Miss Isabella! The man, Heathcliff, gave her father a sovereign* so he has said nothing about what happened, but the daughter has told it all over Gimmerton this morning.'

'But it can't be true,' exclaimed Linton. 'Ellen Dean, go and find her!'

25 I ran upstairs to Isabella's room, knowing already what I would find. I came downstairs and confirmed the servant's words.

'She has gone,' I said, but I did not tell the master I had known for some hours already. I did not dare. 'Are we going 30 to try to find them and bring her back?' I asked.

'She went of her own free will,' answered the master. 'She had the right to go if she wanted to. It is not I that have left her, she has left me. From now on, she is my sister in name only.'

35 And that was all that he said on the subject. He did not make a single enquiry further, but he told me to send the things that she owned to her new house, wherever it was, when I knew it.

*sovereign, English coin at that time.

9 Isabella's Troubles

For two months Heathcliff and Isabella remained absent.
During this time, Mrs Linton suffered and recovered from a
very bad attack of what is called brain fever. No mother could
have nursed an only child more carefully than Edgar looked
after her. Day and night he watched over her and patiently   5
put up with everything. He was full of joy and thankfulness
when he was told Catherine's life was out of danger.

Catherine's health improves

The first time she left her room was at the beginning of the
following March. It was the year 1784, eighteen years ago. Mr
Linton had put on her pillow, in the morning, a handful of   10
golden spring crocuses.* Her eyes caught sight of them as she
woke, and shone with delight as she gathered them eagerly in
her hands.

'These are the earliest flowers at the Heights,' she exclaimed. 'They remind me of soft winds, and warm sunshine,   15
and nearly melted snow. Edgar, isn't there a south wind now,
and hasn't the snow nearly gone?'

'The snow has completely gone down here, darling,' replied
her husband. 'The sky is blue, the birds are singing, and the
streams are full of water from the melting snow from the   20
higher hills. Catherine, last spring at this time I was longing
to have you under this roof. Now I wish you were a mile or
two up those hills. The air blows so sweetly there. I feel it
would cure you completely.'

'I shall never go there again, except for once more!' said   25
Catherine. 'And when I go that time, I shall remain there forever. Next spring you'll long again to have me under this roof,
and you'll look back and think you were happy today.'

On hearing these terrible words, Linton tried to cheer her.

*crocus, a spring flower.

But nothing would amuse her, and she let tears fall down her cheeks.

We knew she was really better, and therefore decided that being in one room for so long could cause this kind of behaviour. But I could not help remembering the doctor's words that her brain might be permanently damaged. 5

Still, I lit the fire in the sitting room, as the master had ordered me to, and said nothing. I placed a chair in the sunshine by the window. Then he brought her down, and she sat for a long time in that spot, enjoying the gentle warmth. By evening, though, she seemed very tired. But no arguments 10 could persuade her to return to her bedroom, so I had to make a bed on the sofa in the sitting room. Then, later, so she did not have to climb the stairs each day, we changed the small room next to the sitting room into a little bedroom 15 for her.

I did think that she was really recovering, and hoped strongly that she was, since now there was a double reason to see her well and strong. Catherine was expecting a child. We all looked forward to the day when Catherine would give Mr 20 Linton a son, and his lands would be safe from a stranger's hands.

Isabella's letter

Some six weeks after Miss Isabella left the house, that terrible night, she sent her brother a short note announcing her marriage to Heathcliff. Linton did not reply to this, I be- 25 lieve. A fortnight later I got a long letter from Isabella which I thought very odd, coming from the pen of a bride who had just finished her honeymoon*.

'Dear Ellen,' she wrote, 'I arrived back at Wuthering Heights last night, and heard for the first time that Catherine has 30 been, and still is, very ill. I must not write to her, I suppose, and my brother is either too angry or too upset to answer what I sent him. Still, I must write to someone at the Grange, so I have chosen you.

*honeymoon, holiday for newly married people.

'Please tell Edgar that I am longing to see him again. Say that my heart returned to Thrushcross Grange twenty-four hours after I left it, and there it is at this moment, full of warm feelings for Catherine and Edgar.

5   'The remainder of this letter is for yourself alone. I want to ask you two questions. The first is, how did you manage to remain a normal, kind human being when you lived here? Of all the people that live here, I cannot find one who has normal decent human feelings.

10   'The second question is this — Is Mr Heathcliff a man? If so, is he mad? And if not, is he a devil? I shan't tell you my reasons for this enquiry, but please explain, if you can, what I have married. You can tell me everything when you call to see me, and you must call very soon. Don't write, but come,

15   and bring me something from Edgar.

'Now you shall hear how I have been welcomed in my new home, as I am told that the Heights is to be our home. It was dark when we arrived in the courtyard of the farm-house, and your old companion, Joseph, came out from one of the out-

20   buildings to welcome us. You can imagine what kind of a welcome that was. His first act was to raise the weak candle he was carrying to my face. He took a long, good look, and then turned away, saying nothing, only muttering. Then he took the two horses we had come on, and led them into the

25   stables. He reappeared only in order to lock the outer gate, as if we were living in an ancient castle.

'Heathcliff stayed outside talking to him for a while, but I entered the kitchen — a small untidy hole. You would not know it, it has changed so much since you left. By the fire

30   stood a dirty looking child, strong, but dressed in terrible rags. He had a look of Catherine in his eyes and mouth.

' "This is Edgar's nephew by marriage," I thought to my-self, "and mine too, now, in a way. I must kiss him, and make a good beginning with him."

35   'I approached, and trying to take his dirty hand in mine and said, "How do you do, dear?"

'He replied in words that I could not understand.

' "Shall you and I be friends, Hareton?" was my next attempt at conversation.

'He swore at me and threatened to set the dog on me if I did not go away immediately. This was the kind of answer I received by trying to be kind!

'I went outside, deciding to enter the house again later, with Heathcliff by my side. I could not see Mr Heathcliff anywhere. Joseph, whom I followed to the stables, started muttering to himself when I asked him to take me inside. He pretended not to understand my way of speaking.

' "I said I want you to come with me into the house!" I cried, thinking that perhaps he was a bit deaf as well, but I was very upset by his rudeness.

' "Not me," he answered. "I've got something else to do," and he went on with his work, ignoring me. I walked round the yard and through a gate to another door, at which I decided to knock. After a short while, it was opened by a tall, thin man, extremely untidy. His face could hardly be seen because of his long stringy hair that hung about his eyes and which reached down to his shoulders. His eyes, too, were rather like Catherine's, except that they had none of her beauty.

' "What's your business here?" he asked harshly. "Who are you?"

' "My name was Isabella Linton," I replied. "You've seen me before, sir. I have just married Mr Heathcliff, and he has brought me here, I suppose with your permission."

' "He has come back, then?" asked the man, staring like a hungry wolf.

' "Yes, we've just arrived," I said. "Heathcliff left me by the kitchen door. When I went in, your little boy played at being a guard and frightened me away by threatening to set a dog on me."

' "It's good that Heathcliff has kept his promise and returned!" growled my future host.

'He frightened me, this brother of Catherine's, and I was sorry that I had tried this second entrance. However, Hindley ordered me inside, and shut and relocked the door. I found myself inside a huge room, lit only by an enormous fire. I asked whether I might call the maid, so that she might show me my bedroom. Mr Earnshaw did not answer this request.

5 He only walked up and down, with his hands in his pockets, apparently quite forgetting me. I was afraid to repeat my question.

'You'll not be surprised, Ellen, that I felt particularly unhappy, seated there in that huge room. I was not alone, it is

10 true, but it was worse than being by myself. I remembered that only four miles away lay my delightful home, containing the only people I loved on earth. And there might as well have been the Atlantic sea between us, instead of those four miles.

15 'I asked myself where I could turn for comfort. You mustn't tell Edgar, or Catherine of this. But above every other sorrow, my greatest despair was that I could find no one at Wuthering Heights who would be my friend against Heathcliff!

20 'I had come to Wuthering Heights almost gladly, because it meant that I would no longer have to live alone with him. But he knew the people we were coming to live amongst, and he did not worry about any interference from them.

'I sat there and thought sadly for quite a long time. The

25 clock struck nine, and we had arrived at about six. My companion was still walking up and down the room, always silent except for an occasional groan, or a bitter word.

'I listened to the noises coming from other parts of the house, but I could not hear a woman's voice at all, although I

30 longed to hear one. Eventually I could bear it all no longer, and I burst into bitter tears.

'I was not aware of how openly I wept, till Earnshaw halted in front of me, and gave me a stare of complete surprise. Taking advantage of his attention, I exclaimed, "I'm

35 tired from my journey, and I want to go to bed! Where is the maid-servant? Tell me where I can find her, since she won't come here!"

' "We have none," he answered. "You must look after yourself."

' "Where am I to sleep, then?" I sobbed. I was too tired and upset to be able to control myself any longer.

' "Joseph will show you Heathcliff's room," he said. "Open   5
that door, Joseph's in there."

Hindley wants to kill Heathcliff

'I was just about to go and find him, when Hindley suddenly stopped me, and said in the strangest voice, "Make sure that you lock the door when you are in Heathcliff's room. Please don't forget!"   10

' "Why, Mr Earnshaw?" I asked, not liking the idea of deliberately locking myself into a room alone with Heathcliff.

' "Look here!" he replied, pulling out a strange gun from underneath his jacket. It had a double-edged knife in it that was attached to the barrel, and would spring out when a little   15
knob was pressed. "I'm going to kill him with this one day. And every night I go up there to his room and try to open the door. If I ever find it open, I shall go in and kill him! When that time comes, not all the angels in heaven shall save him!"   20

'I looked at the weapon curiously. A horrible thought struck me: how powerful I would be if I had such an instrument! I took it from his hand, and touched the blade. He looked astonished at the expression that he saw on my face. He took the gun back quickly, shut the knife and returned it   25
to its hiding place, under his jacket.

' "I don't care if you do tell Heathcliff that I have it," he said. "It'll make him more careful. You will have to watch for him. I see his danger does not shock you."

' "What has Heathcliff done to you?" I asked. "How has he   30
wronged you? Wouldn't it be wiser and easier to ask him to leave the house?"

' "No!" shouted Earnshaw. "If he offers to leave me, he's a dead man. If you persuade him to do that you will become a murderess. Am I to lose all without a chance of trying to   35 get it back? Is Hareton to be a beggar? I will have it all back, and I'll have his gold too, and then his blood, and the devil shall have his soul!"

'You've told me before, Ellen, of your old master's habits. He is quite clearly going mad. He was last night, at least. I was terrified to be near him, and thought of Joseph, in spite of his rudeness, as better company than him.

'As soon as Hindley began marching up and down, I escaped into the kitchen, through the door that Hindley had mentioned earlier.

'Joseph was making porridge* on the fire. I bent over the fire to watch. It looked awful. Crying out sharply, "I'll make that," I took the pot out of his reach, and then took off my hat and coat.

' "Mr Earnshaw," I said, "tells me that I must look after myself. I'm not going to act the lady among you, for fear that I should starve."

'Joseph's mutters had no effect on me. I went quickly to work, though it was rather a mess when I had finished, I must admit. There were four places set at the table. A huge container of fresh milk had been brought into the kitchen. Hareton seized this, and began drinking directly from it, spilling milk everywhere. I was very angry and told him to get a cup, as no one else would want to drink the milk after he had dirtied it like that. Hareton took no notice of me, but went on sucking at the container.

' "I shall have my supper in another room," I said. "Do you have another sitting room?"

' "Sitting room," said Joseph, with a horrid laugh. "We have no sitting room but this and the front room."

' "Then I shall go upstairs," I answered. "Show me my room."

'With many complaints, the man rose and took me upstairs, opening a door now and then, to look into the other rooms that we passed. He halted in front of one, which I thought was probably the best. There was a good carpet, but the

*porridge, a breakfast food.

pattern could hardly be seen under a thick coating of dust. The furniture was expensive and modern, but had obviously not been treated well.

' "This is the master's room," said my stupid guide. When I told him that I wanted a room for myself, to sleep in, Joseph took no notice. He went downstairs again, taking the candle with him. I waited there in the dark. Later, he came upstairs again, with Hareton, and put him to bed.

' "There's room for you both here," he said. I ran down to the kitchen and threw myself into a chair by the fire. Here, weeping quietly to myself, I soon fell asleep.

'Heathcliff woke me up. He had just come in, and demanded, in his loving manner, what I was doing there. I told him that he had the key of our room in his pocket. The adjective "our" made him very angry. He swore it was not, and never would be, mine. But I'll not repeat his language, nor describe his usual behaviour towards myself. Sometimes my curiosity is greater than my fear, yet I tell you that a tiger or a poisonous snake could not terrify me more than he does sometimes.

'He told me of Catherine's illness, and accused my brother of causing it. He promises that I shall suffer instead of Edgar, till he can get hold of Edgar himself.

'I do hate him — and I am so miserable and unhappy — I have been a fool!

'Make sure that you do not repeat any of the letter to the others at the Grange. I shall expect to see you every day. Please do not disappoint me!

'Isabella'

10　Ellen Dean Visits Wuthering Heights

As soon as I had read this letter, I went to the master and
told him that his sister had arrived at the Heights, and had
sent me a letter telling of her sorrow over Mrs Linton's illness.
I said she had an urgent wish to see him. I told him also, that
5　she wished he would send her some little thing as soon as
possible, as a sign of forgiveness.

'Forgiveness!' said Linton. 'I have nothing to forgive her,
Ellen. You may call at the Heights this afternoon, if you like,
and say that I am not angry, and that I am sorry to have lost
10　her, especially as I know that she will be unhappy with Heathcliff. I cannot go to see her, however. If she really wants to
make me happy, tell her to persuade the man she has married
to leave the country.'

'And you won't write her a little note, sir?' I asked, hope-
15　fully.

'No,' he answered. 'I shall neither write nor speak to any
member of Heathcliff's family.'

Isabella looks like a servant

Mr Edgar's coldness made me upset. All the way from the
Grange to Wuthering Heights, I puzzled my brains as to how
20　to soften his refusal of a letter to make Isabella happy. I
entered the house without knocking. Hindley was not there.
Mr Heathcliff sat at a table, but he rose when I appeared and
offered me a chair. He was the only thing that looked decent.
Everything had changed so much since they had returned to
25　Wuthering Heights from their marriage, that it was he who
would have appeared a proper gentleman to a stranger, and
his wife would have seemed a dirty serving maid.

Isabella came forward eagerly to greet me, and held out
one hand to take the expected letter. I shook my head. She
30　would not understand the hint. Heathcliff guessed the

meaning of her movements, and said, 'If you have got anything for Isabella, Nelly, give it to her. You needn't make a
secret of it, we have no secrets between us.'

'Oh, I have nothing,' I replied, thinking it best to speak the
truth at once. 'My master told me to tell you,' I said, speak-   5
ing to Isabella, 'that you must not expect either a letter or a
visit from him.'

Mrs Heathcliff bit at her lip, as if to control her tears at
this news. She returned to her seat in the window. Her husband went and stood near the fire close to me, and began to   10
question me about Catherine. I told him as much as I thought
necessary of her illness. He managed to get from me most of
the facts of how her illness began.

'Before you leave this house,' he said, 'I must have a
promise from you that you'll let me see her. I must see her!   15
What do you say?'

'I say, Mr Heathcliff, that you must not. You never shall,
through me. Another meeting between you and the master
might kill her altogether.'

'With your help, such a meeting could be avoided,' he said.   20
'You know, as well as I do, that for every thought she has for
Linton, she has a thousand for me! I was a fool to think for a
moment that she was more fond of Edgar Linton than of me.
He couldn't love as much in eighty years as I could in a day.
And Catherine has a heart as deep as I have. It is not possible   25
for him to be loved like me. How can she love him for some-
thing he does not have?'

'Catherine and Edgar are as fond of each other as any two
people can be,' cried Isabella, with sudden courage. 'I won't
sit silent and hear my brother being spoken of like that.'   30

'Your brother is wonderfully fond of you too, isn't he?'
said Heathcliff scornfully. 'He has let you loose on the world
with remarkable speed.'

'He is not aware of what I suffer,' she replied. 'I did not
tell him that.'   35

'You have been telling him something, then. You have
written?'

'To say that I was married, I did write that, you saw the note.'

'And nothing since?'

'No.'

5 'My lady is looking very unhappy,' I said. 'Somebody does not love her much I should think. Who that is I can guess, but perhaps I shouldn't say.'

'I should guess it is her own fault,' said Heathcliff. 'She has begun to look like something worse than a kitchen servant! 10 She no longer tries to please me at all. Still, she'll suit this house so much the better for not being too grand, and I'll take care that she does not disgrace me by going outside and being seen.'

Heathcliff continued to say the most horrible things about 15 Mrs Heathcliff until I could bear it no longer.

'Mr Heathcliff,' I said, 'this is the talk of a madman, and your wife, most likely, is certain that you are mad. That is why she has stayed here with you. But now that you say she may leave, I am sure she will.' I turned to Isabella, 'Surely, 20 madam you will not stay here any longer?'

'Take care, Ellen!' said Isabella, her eyes sparkling angrily. She obviously no longer loved him. 'Don't believe a single word he says. He is a lying devil, and not a human being at all. He has said that I can leave, and I've tried, but I dare not 25 repeat it! But Ellen, promise that you'll not mention any of this conversation to my brother or Catherine. Whatever Heathcliff may pretend, all he wishes to do is to make Edgar desperate. He says he has married me only to get some power over Edgar, but he shall not get it. I'd rather die first! The 30 single pleasure I can imagine is to die, or to see him dead!'

Heathcliff dismisses Isabella

'Go upstairs!' ordered Heathcliff. 'Go upstairs immediately, I wish to speak to Ellen Dean alone.' He seized her and pushed her from the room.

I decided I had seen enough for one day, and picked up 35 my hat.

'Put that down!' Heathcliff said angrily. 'You are not going yet. Come here now, Nelly. I must either persuade you, or make you help me to see Catherine as soon as possible. I swear that I mean no harm. I don't wish to cause any trouble, or to upset Mr Linton. I only wish to hear from Catherine 5 herself, how she is, and why she has been ill, and to ask if I could do anything of use to her. Last night, I was in the Grange garden for six hours, and I'll return there tonight, and every night till I find an opportunity to enter. If Edgar Linton meets me, I shall not hesitate to knock him down. If his 10 servants get in my way, I shall threaten them with these guns. But wouldn't it be better to prevent my coming into contact with them or their master? And you could do it so easily. I'd warn you when I was coming, and then you could let me in without anyone else seeing, as soon as she was alone, and 15 then watch until I left. You would be preventing trouble.'

I disliked the thought of playing such a part in my employer's house. I pointed out the cruelty and selfishness of his destroying Mrs Linton's peace for his own satisfaction.

'The most ordinary things upset her,' I said. 'She is so 20 nervous that she couldn't bear the surprise, I'm sure. Don't talk about it, please, or I will have to tell the master what you intend doing so that he can be prepared against you.'

'If you do that, I'll make sure that you do not leave this house until tomorrow evening,' declared Heathcliff. 'Let us 25 decide at once, will you stay here, and am I to fight my way to Catherine, over Linton and his servants? Or will you be my friend, as you have been up to now, and do what I ask? Decide now, because there is no reason for me to stay another minute if you insist on being unhelpful and difficult.' 30

I argued and complained, and refused to help him fifty times, but finally he forced me to agree with him. I agreed to carry a letter from him to the mistress. If she consented, I promised to let him know when Linton was next absent from home, so that he would be able to come to see Catherine un- 35 noticed. I would make sure that I and all the other servants would be out of the way.

Was I right, or wrong? I am afraid I was wrong, but I thought, too, that it might help Catherine's mental illness.

My journey home to the Grange was sadder than my journey to the Heights, and I had many doubts before I could 5 make myself put Heathcliff's letter into Mrs Linton's hand.

11   A Birth and a Death

That evening, after my visit to the Heights, I knew, even though I could not see him, that Heathcliff was near the Grange somewhere. I did not want to go out, in case I saw him, because I still carried his letter in my pocket. I did not want to be threatened or bothered any more. I had decided   *5* not to give the letter to Catherine until my master had gone out somewhere, because I could not guess how the contents of the letter would affect Catherine. As a result of all this, the letter did not reach her until three days later. I gave it to her on a Sunday, after the family had gone to church.   *10*

Mrs Linton sat in a loose, white dress in the window seat, where she usually liked to sit. Her appearance was changed, as I had told Heathcliff, but when she was calm there seemed a strange beauty in the change. The flash of her eyes had been replaced by a dreamy softness. They appeared to look   *15* on things beyond this world. The paleness of her face added to the delicate feeling which surrounded her. She looked like one who is about to decay.

Gimmerton church bells were still ringing, and the flow of the stream in the valley could be heard through the open   *20* window. At Wuthering Heights these sounds could always be heard on quiet days, and it was of Wuthering Heights that Catherine was now thinking as she listened to the familiar sounds.

'There's a letter for you, Mrs Linton,' I said, gently putting   *25* it into the hand that rested on her knee. 'You must read it immediately, because it must be answered.' She did not take any notice for a long time, so I added, 'Must I read it, madam? It is from Heathcliff.'

There was a start of surprise, and a troubled look of   *30* recognition. She lifted the letter and seemed to read it.

'He wishes to see you,' I said. 'He's in the garden now and waiting to know what answer I shall bring.'

Heathcliff enters the house

The next minute I heard a step in the hall. The open house was too inviting for Heathcliff to be able to wait outside. In a
5 step or two he was at her side, and held her in his arms.

He neither spoke nor loosened his hold for some five minutes. I could see from his face, which was full of sadness, that he knew, as I did, that there was no possibility of recovery for Catherine. She would soon die.

10 'O Cathy! Oh, my life! How can I bear it?' he spoke in a tone that could not hide his despair.

'What is this?' said Catherine, leaning back and looking at him with a frown. 'You and Edgar have broken my heart, Heathcliff! And now you come here and tell me of it, as if
15 you were the one to be pitied! I shall not pity you, not I. You have killed me. How strong you are! How many years do you mean to live after I have gone? I wish I could keep hold of you until we were both dead! I shouldn't care what you suffered. I care nothing for your sufferings. Why shouldn't
20 you suffer? I do! Will you forget me? Will you be happy when I am in the earth? Will you say twenty years from now, "That is the grave of Catherine Earnshaw. I loved her long ago, but it is past." Will you think like that, Heathcliff?'

'Don't speak like that to me, Catherine, or I'll become as
25 mad as you are.' He cried, shaking his head.

To a stranger the two would have made a strange and fearful picture. All the blood had left Catherine's face. Her eyes were huge and wild. She looked cold and cruel. Her companion had taken her arm with one hand, and when he let go, I
30 could see clear marks, left blue in her colourless skin.

'Have you a devil in you,' he asked angrily, 'to talk in that manner to me when you are dying? All those words will remain in my memory long after you have left me! While you are at peace, I shall remember every word and be in hell*.'

*hell, the opposite of heaven.

'I shall not be at peace,' cried Catherine. 'I'm not wishing you a greater hurt than I have, Heathcliff. I only wish that we shall never be parted. If any word of mine hurts you afterwards, you may think that I feel the same hurt underneath, and, for my own sake, forgive me!' 5

Heathcliff went back to her chair and leant over her, but so that she could not see his face, which was clouded with sorrow.

'I'm tired of being trapped in this broken prison of a body,' she continued. 'I'm tired and I wish to escape into that world 10 beyond the grave. Heathcliff, dear, you should not be sad now. Do come to me Heathcliff.'

In her eagerness she rose and supported herself on the arm of the chair. When she spoke those heartbreaking words to him, he turned to her, looking absolutely desperate. His eyes 15 were wide and full of unwept tears. Catherine made a spring, and he caught her, and he held her as though he would never let her go alive. I did not feel that I was in the company of normal human beings, so strong did their feelings seem to be.

'Ah, Cathy,' cried Heathcliff, 'why did you marry Linton?' 20

'If I've done wrong,' sobbed Catherine, 'I'm dying for it. You left me too, you remember, all those years ago. I won't scold you now for it. I forgive you. Forgive me.'

'It is hard to forgive,' he answered, 'and to look at those eyes, and feel those thin hands. Don't let me see your eyes. I 25 forgive what you have done to me. I love my murderer. But how can I love yours?'

They were silent, their faces hidden against each other. I grew uncomfortable, for the afternoon was passing quickly, and I could hear people leaving from Gimmerton church 30 already.

'The church service is over,' I said. 'Mr Linton will be back in half an hour.'

Heathcliff swore softly and held Catherine closer. She never moved. Before long Mr Linton opened the gate. 35

'Now he is here!' I exclaimed. 'For heaven's sake hurry away. You won't meet anyone if you go down the front stairs.'

'I must go, Cathy,' said Heathcliff. 'But if I live, I'll see you again before I sleep. I won't go five yards from your window.'

'You must not go!' she answered, holding him as firmly as her strength allowed. 'You shall not, I tell you.'   5

'I must, Linton will be coming up immediately.'

He would have gone then, but there was a look of mad determination on her face.

'No!' she shrieked. 'Oh, don't, don't go! It is the last time I shall see you. Edgar will not hurt us. Heathcliff, I shall die!'   10

'Here comes the fool!' cried Heathcliff, sinking back into a chair. 'Hush, my darling! Hush, Catherine, I'll stay. If he shoots me while I am sitting here, I'd die happy.'

I heard my master climbing the stairs. A cold sweat ran down from my forehead. I was horrified.   15

'Are you going to listen to her mad words?' I asked. 'She doesn't know what she is saying. You must go before we are all ruined. Get up! We will all be in trouble — master, mistress and servant.'

Catherine faints

I cried out with fear and anger, and Mr Linton hurried as   20
he heard the noise. Then I noticed that Catherine had gone limp.

'She's fainted or dead,' I thought. 'So much the better. Far better that she should be dead, than continue to be a burden and a misery-maker to all around her.'   25

Edgar rushed into the room, taking in the scene with one look. What he meant to do I cannot tell. However Heathcliff prevented him doing anything at once by placing the lifeless-looking body in his arms.

'Look there!' he said. 'Unless you are a devil, help her first,   30
then you can speak to me!'

He walked out. Mr Linton called me, and we managed to make Catherine recover from her faint, but she could not recognize anyone. She only groaned and muttered to herself. Edgar in his anxiety, forgot her hated friend. I did not, and   35

at the first opportunity I went outside and found him, told
him that Catherine was better and that he could go. I would
tell him the next morning how she was.

'I will stay and wait in the garden,' he answered, 'and,
5　Nelly, make sure that you do not forget to come and tell me
tomorrow. I shall be waiting under those trees over there.'

Catherine dies

About twelve o'clock that night, the Catherine who now
lives at Wuthering Heights was born. Two hours after she was
born, the mother died. It was eighteen years ago, but like
10　yesterday to me.

It was an unwelcome child, born three months early, and
could easily have died those first few hours of its life, poor
thing.

Next morning, it was bright and cheerful out of doors. The
15　room was silent. The bed, and the person in it were covered
by a soft, tender light. The master looked asleep, next to his
dead wife. She looked as beautiful as an angel in heaven. I
shall never forget how calm she looked.

I decided to go outside into the fresh air, at least that is
20　what I wanted the other servants to think. My chief reason
was to find Heathcliff. I wished, yet feared to find him. I felt
the terrible news must be told, but how to do it I did not
know. He was there, where he said he would be, leaning
against an old tree. His hat was off and his hair was wet from
25　the earlier rain. He had been standing a long time in that position, for I saw a pair of birds passing hardly three feet from
him. They flew off at my approach, and he raised his eyes
and spoke.

'She's dead!' he said. 'I know it already, I've not waited for
30　you to tell me that. Put your handkerchief away. She wants
none of your tears!'

I was weeping as much for him as for her.

'Yes, she's dead,' I answered, stopping my tears. 'She has
gone to heaven, I hope, where we may all join her, if we take
35　warning, and leave our evil ways.'

'Did she take warning, then?' asked Heathcliff. 'Did she die
like a saint? Come, tell me exactly how she died.'

He tried to say her name, but he could not. He kept his
sorrow inside himself. His pride would not let him grieve
openly.   5

'She died as quietly as a lamb,' I said. 'She drew in a sigh,
and stretched herself like a child, and then seemed to sink
into sleep again. Then, five minutes later, I could see that her
heart was no longer beating.'

'And did she ever mention me?' he asked, hesitating, as if   10
he feared that the answer to his question would introduce
details that he could not bear to hear.

'Her senses never returned after you left her,' I said. 'She
recognized nobody. She lies there now with a sweet smile on
her face, she must have been thinking of the early, pleasant   15
days. Her life ended in a gentle dream. I hope she wakes as
kindly in the other world!'

'I hope not!' he cried with terrible anger. 'Why, she is a liar
to the very end! Where is she? Not there, not in heaven.
Catherine Earnshaw, may you not rest as long as I am living!   20
You said I killed you, haunt* me then! I know that ghosts
have wandered on earth. O God! It is awful! I cannot live
without my soul!'

Then he noticed me watching him, so he shouted a com-
mand at me to go, and I obeyed. It was beyond my skill to   25
quieten or help him.

The funeral

It was decided that Mrs Linton's funeral would take place
on the Friday following her death. Linton spent his days and
nights beside the open coffin. Heathcliff spent his nights outside, never sleeping. On the Tuesday, a little after dark, my   30
master, from complete tiredness, had been forced to go to
sleep for a few hours. I went and opened one of the windows
to call to Heathcliff, so that he should have a chance of saying one final goodbye.

*haunt, visit (of ghosts).

He took advantage of the opportunity, quietly and quickly, so that no one but I knew that he had come.

Mr Earnshaw was, of course, invited to attend his sister's funeral. He sent no excuse and he did not come. The place 5 that Catherine was buried, to the surprise of the villagers, was neither in the church under the carved stone of the Lintons, nor by the graves of her own relatives outside. Her grave was dug on a green slope in a corner of the churchyard, where the wall is so low that the wild moorland flowers have climbed 10 over it. Only a few stones separated her from the moor itself.

12   Isabella Leaves Wuthering Heights

The next day the wind changed direction, bringing rain first
and then snow. My master stayed in his room. I went into the
lonely sitting room, and was sitting with the crying child on
my knee and watching the snowflakes outside the window,
when someone entered, out of breath and laughing. My anger   *5*
was greater than my astonishment for a minute. I thought it
was one of the maids, and I cried, 'How dare you behave in
that manner here? What would Mr Linton say if he heard
you?'

'Excuse me,' answered a familiar voice, 'but I know Edgar   *10*
is in bed, and I cannot help it.'

With that, the speaker came forward to the fire, gasping
and holding her side.

'I have run all the way from Wuthering Heights,' she continued, after a pause, 'I couldn't count the number of falls   *15*
I've had. Don't be alarmed! I will give you an explanation as
soon as I get my breath back. Only, please be kind enough to
step outside and order the carriage to take me to Gimmerton,
and tell a servant to find a few clothes from my cupboard.'

The strange figure that stood before me was Mrs Heathcliff.   *20*
She did not look as though she had anything to laugh about.
Her hair had fallen in a ragged wet mess around her shoulders,
dripping snow and water onto the floor. Her dress stuck to
her wetly, and her feet were covered only in thin slippers.

'My dear young lady,' I exclaimed, 'I'll not move from this   *25*
spot until you have changed your clothes, and put on dry
things. Certainly, you will not go to Gimmerton tonight, so
it is quite unnecessary to order the carriage.'

'Certainly I shall,' she said, 'but I have no objection to
dressing myself decently.'   *30*

She insisted that I did as I was told before she would let
me touch her. It was not until the coachman had been in-

structed to get ready, and a maid sent to pack some necessary clothes, that I obtained permission to change what she was wearing.

'Now, Ellen,' she said, when I had finished, and she had
5   seated herself in a comfortable chair near the fire, 'bring me a cup of tea, and then sit down here opposite me, and put poor Catherine's baby away. I don't want to see it. You mustn't think that I don't care about Catherine. I've cried bitterly, but I was not going to sympathize with Heathcliff, the hor-
10 rible beast!' She slipped the gold ring from her wedding finger and dropped it into the fire.

'Heathcliff is a monster!'

I asked her why she had escaped from Wuthering Heights.

'I should, and wish to remain here,' answered Isabella, 'but I tell you, he wouldn't let me. Do you think he could bear to
15 see me grow well and happy, could bear to think that we were living in peace, and not wish to destroy our happiness? He has succeeded completely in making me hate him. Yet I can still remember how I loved him. But even if he had loved me, his horrible nature would have made itself known some-
20 how. Catherine must have been very odd to like him so well, knowing what he was like. Monster!'

'Hush, hush! He's a human being,' I said. 'Be a little more kind. There are worse men than him in the world.'

'He's not a human being,' she replied, 'and he has no right
25 to expect kindness from me. I gave him my heart, and he took it and pinched it to death, and then threw it back to me. Because it has been finally destroyed, I no longer have the power to feel for him. I cannot, not even if he cried from now to his dying day, and wept tears of blood for Catherine! You
30 asked me what has driven me to escape at last? I was forced to try, because I had succeeded in making him so angry that he tried to kill me.

'Yesterday, you know, Mr Earnshaw should have gone to the funeral. He kept himself sober* so that he could attend,

sober, not drunk.

fairly sober, anyway. He did not go to bed mad at six o'clock, and get up drunk at twelve. But, because he had not been drinking as usual, he got up feeling very unhappy. So instead of going to church, he sat down by the fire and swallowed brandy.

'Heathcliff (I tremble at his name) has been a stranger in the house from last Sunday until today. He has not eaten a meal with us for nearly a week. All last week he would come home at dawn, and go straight upstairs to his room, locking himself inside. Then he would be off again in the afternoon, always straight back down to the Grange! I am surprised that Edgar did not send for the police, and have him sent to prison.

'But although I was upset by Catherine's death, it was almost like a holiday not to have Heathcliff in the house swearing at me. I could even listen to Joseph without bursting into tears. You wouldn't think that I could cry at anything Joseph said. But he and Hareton are such horrible companions that I'd rather sit with Hindley, and hear his awful talk, than with the little boy and that horrible old man. When Heathcliff is in, I'm often forced to go into the kitchen with them, or starve among the damp, unused rooms in the rest of the house.

'So, yesterday evening, I sat in my corner by the fire reading some old books until twelve o'clock. It seemed so cold to go upstairs, with the wind and wild snow blowing outside. My thoughts were continually turning to the churchyard and the newly made grave. Hindley sat opposite me, his head leaning on his hand, perhaps thinking of the same subject. He had stopped drinking, but had neither moved nor spoken for three hours. There was no sound in the house except the wind whistling round the corners and the sound of burning logs in the fire. Hareton and Joseph were probably asleep in bed.

Hindley locks out Heathcliff

'The miserable silence was broken, in the end, by the sound of someone trying to open the kitchen door. Heathcliff

had returned from his watch earlier than usual, because, I
suppose, of the sudden storm. However, the kitchen door was
locked, and we heard him coming round to get in by the
other entrance. My companion looked at me.

5 ' "I'll keep him outside for five minutes," he exclaimed.
"You won't object?"

' "No. You may keep him out the whole night for me," I
answered. "Yes, do! Put the key in the lock, and turn it,
quickly!"

10 'Earnshaw did this, before Heathcliff had reached the front.
He then came to me looking for sympathy to match the burning hate that he was feeling. He found enough sympathy to
encourage him to speak.

' "You and I have a great debt to settle with that man out
15 there! Are you as soft as your brother, or will you help me
now in trying to repay some of the wrongs he has done us?
All I ask you to do, Mrs Heathcliff, is to sit still and say
nothing. He'll cause your death and my ruin if I don't act
now. Listen to him, he knocks at the door as if he were
20 master here already! Promise to be silent, and before that
clock strikes − there are only three minutes left till one
o'clock − you'll be a free woman!"

'He took the weapons which I described to you in my
letter, from under his jacket, and would have put out the
25 candle, if I had let him. I grabbed it away from him, however,
and seized his arm.

' "I'll not be silent," I said. "You mustn't touch him. Let
the door remain shut, and be quiet."

' "No, I've decided to do this, and by God I will!" cried
30 the desperate Hindley. "I'll do you this kindness in spite of
yourself, and do justice for Hareton! You needn't trouble to
protect me. Catherine is gone, and there is no one left now
who would miss me. It's time to make an end!"

'I might as well have reasoned with a madman. The only
35 thing left for me to do was to run to a window, and warn his
intended victim of what was planned for him.

' "You'd better stay somewhere else tonight," I shouted,

in rather a triumphant voice. "Mr Earnshaw has decided to shoot you."

' "You'd better open the door, you —," he answered, addressing me by a word that I don't care to repeat.

' "I shall not help you further," I shouted. "Come in and 5 get shot if you please. I've done my duty."

'I shut the window, and returned to my place by the fire. Hindley swore angrily at me, saying that I still loved the man. Secretly, I thought what a blessing it would be for him, if Heathcliff would put him out of his misery, and what a bless- 10 ing it would be for me, if Hindley would kill Heathcliff!

'As I sat there, thinking these thoughts, the window behind me broke all over the floor, and Heathcliff's face looked through. He tried to get in, but his shoulders were too broad, and I smiled, thinking I was safe from him. His hair and 15 clothes were whitened by the snow. He looked like a monster.

' "Isabella, let me in, or I'll make you sorry!" he cried.

' "I cannot help a murderer," I replied. "Mr Hindley is standing there with a knife and a gun, waiting for you."

' "Let me in by the kitchen door," he said. 20

' "Hindley will get there before I can," I answered, "and that's a poor love of yours that cannot bear a shower of snow! Heathcliff, if I were you, I'd go and stretch myself over Catherine's grave and die like a faithful dog. I can't imagine how you can bear to survive her loss." 25

' "He's there, is he?" shouted Hindley. "If I can get my arm out, I can hit him!"

Hindley fails to kill Heathcliff

'I'm afraid, Ellen, that you must think that I'm really wicked, even though I didn't actually help in trying to kill him. I did wish that he were dead, and therefore I was dis- 30 appointed, and terrified, after what I had said to him, when he threw himself on Earnshaw's weapon, and tore it from his hand.

'The gun went off, and the knife, in springing out, went into its owner's wrist. Heathcliff pulled it out quickly, tear- 35

ing the flesh as he did so, and pushed it into his pocket still
dripping. He then took a stone, and broke the window completely. He jumped into the room without any trouble at all.
Hindley had fallen to the floor, fainting from the pain and
5   the loss of blood. Heathcliff kicked at him as he lay there.
He was holding me all the time, with one hand, to prevent me
from running to Joseph for help. Getting out of breath, he
finally stopped, and dragged the lifeless body to the sofa.
Then he tore off Earnshaw's jacket sleeve, and tied his wound
10   with it. He had freed me to do this, and I lost no time in running away and finding the old servant.

  ' "So, you've tried to murder him!" exclaimed Joseph to
Heathcliff, when he saw Earnshaw's body lying on the sofa.
"I've never seen a sight like this before!" he cried, lifting his
15   hands to his eyes in horror.

  'Heathcliff pushed him to his knees in the middle of the
blood. "Wash that away," he said, and threw a towel at him.
Then he shook me till my teeth ached, and threw me beside
Joseph. "You can help him too. You like this sort of work!"
20   he added.

  'Joseph was finally persuaded that Heathcliff had not
started the fight, and Mr Earnshaw soon showed that he was
still alive. Heathcliff advised Mr Earnshaw to go to bed with
a bottle of brandy. After giving him this advice, Heathcliff
25   left us. Hindley stretched himself out beside the fire. I was
able to go up to my own room unhurt. I was amazed that I
had been able to escape so easily.

  'This morning, when I came down, about half an hour before noon, Mr Earnshaw was sitting by the fire, very sick.
30   Heathcliff, looking almost as bad, was leaning against the
chimney. Neither appeared to want any food, so I ate alone.
Hindley wanted some water, and I handed him a glass, and
asked him how he was.

  ' "Not as ill as I would like," he replied. "Every inch of me
35   is as sore as if I had been fighting with a hundred devils."

  ' "Yes, that's not surprising," I said. "Catherine used to
boast that she stood between you and bodily harm, and it

was true. Last night, only hours after she was dead, Heathcliff kicked and beat you while you lay on the floor. At the Grange everyone knows that your sister would still be alive, if it weren't for Mr Heathcliff."

' "Get up, and get out of my sight," said Heathcliff.   5

' "I beg your pardon," I replied, "but I loved Catherine too, and her brother requires help, which, for her sake, I shall supply. Now that she's dead, I see her in Hindley – "

' "Get up, you horrible fool, before I stamp you to death!" he cried.   10

' "If poor Catherine had trusted you and had become your wife, she would never have allowed you to behave in the awful way that you do."

'Earnshaw and the sofa were between me and Heathcliff. Instead of trying to reach me, he grabbed at a knife on the   15 table and threw it at my head. The last I saw of him, was him rushing at me, and being stopped by Hindley. Then they both fell together on the kitchen floor. In my flight through the kitchen I ordered Joseph to go to his master. I knocked over Hareton, and I jumped, leaped, and flew down the steep road.   20 Then I left it, and went directly across the moor, rolling over banks, and splashing through streams, taking myself as fast as I could towards the Grange. I would rather be forced to live in hell than to stay beneath the roof of Wuthering Heights again even for one night.'   25

The birth of Linton

Isabella stopped speaking, and took a drink of tea. Then she rose, and refusing to listen to me, walked out of the kitchen and got into the waiting carriage. She was driven away, and never revisited this neighbourhood. Later on, she and the master wrote to each other regularly. Her new home   30 was in the south, near London, and there she had a son, born a few months after her escape. The child's name was Linton, and from the first, she wrote to us that he was a weak, unhealthy creature.

Mr Heathcliff, meeting me one day in the village, asked me   35

where she was living. I refused to tell him. He said that it didn't really matter where she lived, except that he would never allow her to live undisturbed near her brother. Later, through the other servants, I think, he discovered where she
5　was and about the existence of the child. Keeping his promise, he didn't go near her and worry her. He often asked about the child, when he saw me, and on being told its name, he smiled grimly, and said, 'They wish me to hate it, too, do they?'

10　'I don't think they wish you to know anything about it,' I answered.

'But, I'll have it when I want it,' he said. 'I'm sure they realize that.'

Fortunately the child's mother died before that time ar-
15　rived. It was some thirteen years after Catherine had died, when young Linton was twelve, or perhaps a little more. That was in 1797, about five years ago.

13   Little Cathy

My master, Mr Edgar Linton, stopped working and going to church. He avoided the village on all occasions, and spent his life alone, seeing no one. He often went for long walks on the moors, or visited the grave of his wife, mostly in the evening, or early morning, before other people were around.   *5*

But, he still had another person to care for and love on earth. By the end of April, the little girl that he had taken no notice of when she was first born, became very precious to him.

He never called her Catherine in full, as he had never called   *10*
the first Catherine by her shorter name, probably because Heathcliff had done so.

The death of Hindley

The end of Earnshaw was what might have been expected. His death quickly followed his sister's. There was hardly six   *15*
months between them. 'He died drunk,' Dr Kenneth told me. I could not help wondering if he had been treated fairly. Whatever I did, that question would bother me, so I asked permission to go to Wuthering Heights to help to get Hindley Earnshaw ready for his own funeral. Mr Linton didn't want   *20*
me to go, but I reminded him that the child, Hareton, was his wife's nephew. Since he was the closest relative, he ought to look after him. I persuaded him that it was his duty to look into the affairs of his brother-in-law. He eventually agreed, but because he still did not feel strong enough to do it him-   *25*
self, he allowed me to go to the Heights to find out what I could. Linton's lawyer had also been Hindley's, so I decided to call in at his home in the village first.

'Hareton's father died in debt,' said the lawyer. 'Money has been borrowed to the full value of the property. The only   *30*

chance for his son is to create some interest in the heart of
Heathcliff, who lent Hindley all the money.'

When I reached the Heights, Mr Heathcliff said he could
not see why I had come, but that I could stay and help make
5 the arrangements for the funeral if I wanted.

'If you want my opinion,' he continued, 'that fool's body
should be buried out on the moors, without a church cere-
mony of any kind. I happened to leave him for ten minutes
yesterday afternoon, and in that time he had locked all the
10 doors so that I couldn't get to him, and he spent the whole
night in drinking himself to death on purpose. We broke in
this morning, and there he was, stretched over the sofa. I sent
for Dr Kenneth, but Hindley was already cold and dead.'

I insisted that the funeral must be respectable. Mr Heath-
15 cliff said I could do as I pleased, only he warned me to remember that the money for the whole affair was coming
from him.

Just before the funeral, Heathcliff lifted the unfortunate
Hareton on to the table, and muttered with peculiar eager-
20 ness, 'Now my good child, you are mine! And I'll see if I can
make this tree grow as crooked as the last, with the same
wind to twist it!' The poor child could not understand the
meaning of these words, but was pleased with the attention
that Heathcliff showed him. He played with the wicked man's
25 hair, and stroked his cheek. I however, understood more
clearly what Heathcliff meant, and said quickly, 'That boy
must go back with me to Thrushcross Grange, sir. There is
nothing in the world less yours than Hareton!'

'Does Linton agree to that?' he demanded.

30 'Of course — he has ordered me to bring him back,' I
replied.

'Well,' answered Heathcliff, 'we'll not argue about it now,
but I have decided I want to have this child, especially since
Linton wants him! I won't let him go easily. In fact if Linton
35 wants him, he'll have to come and get him! Remember to tell
him that.'

This of course prevented all my plans. I told Mr Linton of what had happened, but nothing could persuade him to go into the house where Heathcliff lived.

Heathcliff is the owner of Wuthering Heights

The guest was now the master of Wuthering Heights. This was proved by the lawyer, who in his turn proved it to Mr 5 Linton, that Earnshaw had borrowed heavily in order to play at cards, and he had borrowed from Heathcliff.

In that manner, Hareton, who should have been one of the finest gentlemen in the neighbourhood, was made totally dependent on his father's oldest and most hated enemy. He 10 now lives in his own house like a servant, but he is not even paid any wages. He is quite unable to improve himself because of his lack of friends, and the fact that he does not know that he has been wrongly treated.

Little Cathy was the most beautiful and happy child that 15 ever brought sunshine into a sad house. She had a lovely face, with the Earnshaws' dark eyes, but the Lintons' fair skin and small features and yellow curling hair. She had high spirits, but was not rough, and had a sweet heart that was very loving. In some ways, she reminded me greatly of her mother. 20 She could be so loving, but she did not have the same temper as her mother, for she could be as soft and sweet as a dove, and she had a gentle voice and thoughtful expression. Her anger was never like her mother's either. However, she had her faults, especially a strong will, that children who are 25 spoilt by their parents nearly always have.

Until she reached the age of thirteen, she had not once been out of the Grange property by herself. Mr Linton would take her with him a mile or two outside, on rare occasions, but he trusted her to no one else. Gimmerton was only a 30 name to her, she had never been there. Wuthering Heights and Mr Heathcliff did not exist for her. She was a complete stranger to the outside world. She seemed happy, but sometimes, when looking out at the country from her window, she would say, 'Ellen, how long will it be before I can walk to the 35

top of those hills by myself? I wonder what is on the other
side. Is it the sea? There is so much out there I have never
seen, I will ask father if I can go.'

She did ask him, many times, but the answer was always
5   the same, 'No, not yet Cathy, not yet.' He was terrified that
such walks would bring her into contact with Heathcliff, and
that was a thought that he could not bear.

Edgar visits Isabella

Mrs Isabella Heathcliff lived only about a dozen years after
leaving her husband. Like her brother, she did not have the
10   strong health that is generally found in this area. I am not
certain what her last illness was, but I think it was the same
kind of fever that eventually killed her brother. It started
slowly, but could not be cured and so ended in death as the
patient became weaker and weaker.

15   She wrote to tell her brother that she did not think she
would live much longer, and she asked him to come to her,
if possible. She had a lot to say to him, and she especially
wished to say goodbye to him, and to give him her son,
Linton. She hoped that he would look after Linton. She tried
20   to convince herself that his father would have no wish to take
on the worries of raising a child he obviously did not want,
nor love.

My master did not hesitate to go to her, though he usually
hated to leave home for ordinary things. He left Cathy in my
25   care while he was away, and repeated his orders that she must
not be allowed out onto the moors, even with me. He did not
imagine that she would ever think to go out alone.

He was away three weeks. For the first two days, Cathy
was too sad for either reading or playing, and while she was
30   like that, she caused me no trouble at all. Then, this quiet
behaviour changed, and the child became impatient and
bored. I tried amusing her by letting her ride her pony around
the property, which was quite large. Sometimes she did the
same thing on foot, and used to come back and make up all
35   sorts of things she had seen and heard.

It was mid-summer. Cathy seemed to like the new amusement I had thought of, for she often remained out from
breakfast till teatime. Then the evenings were spent in telling
her stories. I did not fear that she would go outside the gates,
even if they were open. Unluckily I was wrong.   *5*

Cathy goes to Wuthering Heights

Catherine had come down early that morning, at eight
o'clock, and said that she wanted to be an Arab trader that
day. She was going to cross the desert, and I must give her
a lot of food for herself and her animals. She would take a
horse and three camels. These were represented by one large   *10*
dog and a couple of smaller ones.

I collected a large quantity of food, and put it all in a bag,
which I tied on one side of her saddle. She jumped onto her
pony very happily, and went off with a merry laugh.

The naughty child never came to tea that afternoon. One   *15*
traveller, the large dog, which was rather old, came back. But
neither Cathy, nor her pony, nor the two other dogs could
be seen in any direction. Finally, I sent out all the servants to
look for her, and I searched as well.

I saw a workman mending a fence near the road, so I   *20*
decided to ask him if he had seen my little mistress.

'I saw her this morning,' he replied. 'She asked me to cut
her a branch to use for a whip, then she jumped her pony
over the hedge, and galloped out of sight.'

You can guess how I felt when I heard this. I thought she   *25*
had probably gone up past Wuthering Heights, to the hill
beyond, which she so often talked about. 'What will have
happened to her? Perhaps she has slipped and fallen somewhere,' I thought to myself. 'Or perhaps she has been killed,
or broken some of her bones?' I was really worried. I was   *30*
hurrying past the Heights, when I saw a woman there whom
I knew. She had been a servant there since the death of Mr
Earnshaw.

'Ah,' she said, 'you have come to look for your little
mistress! Don't look so frightened. She's here, quite safe. But   *35*
still, I must say, I'm glad you're not the master.'

'Mr Heathcliff's not at home then?' I asked hopefully.

'No, no,' she replied, 'both he and Joseph are out. Come in and rest a little while.'

Cathy is talking to Hareton

I entered, and saw the child who had caused me so much worry. She was seated by the fire, rocking herself in a little 5 chair which had been her mother's when she had been a child. Her hat was hanging on a hook on the wall, and she seemed perfectly at home. She was laughing and talking to Hareton. He was now a great strong lad of eighteen, who stared at her with much curiosity and astonishment. He understood little 10 of what she said, because she spoke so fast, and in an accent* quite different from his own.

'Very well, miss,' I exclaimed, hiding my joy at finding her under a stern face. 'This is your last ride till your father comes back. I'll not trust you to go out alone again, you naughty, 15 naughty girl!'

'Aha, Ellen!' she cried happily, jumping up and running to my side. 'And so you've discovered what I have been doing when I go out alone. Have you ever been here in your life before?' 20

'Put that hat on, and come home at once,' I said. 'I shall not be wanting to hear any more of your stories of where you've been. You've been very, very naughty, Miss Cathy. Remember that Mr Linton told me especially that you were not to go outside the Grange, and now you've run off like 25 this!'

'What have I done?' she sobbed, instantly upset. 'Papa didn't tell me, Ellen. Surely he won't scold me?'

'Come, come,' I said, 'stop that crying. Oh, really, you are thirteen years old, and crying like a baby.' 30

'Don't be too hard on the child, Ellen Dean,' said the servant. 'We made her stop, she wanted to go on. I was afraid that you wouldn't like that. It is so wild up there in those hills.'

accent, method of pronunciation.

Hareton, during this speech, stood there with his hands in his pockets, too awkward to speak. He looked as if he was not pleased to see me, breaking in on his friendly conversation with Cathy.

5 'How long must I wait for you, Cathy?' I continued. 'It will be dark in ten minutes. Where is your pony?'

'It's in the stables,' she answered, and turned to Hareton. 'Please get my horse for me.' She did not know he was her cousin. I suppose she thought him to be a working lad. But

10 in any case, Hareton objected to her tone of voice, for he grew angry.

'I'll not be treated as your servant!' he shouted.

'You'll not what?' asked the astonished Cathy. She recovered from her bad temper, which had caused her to speak

15 sharply in the first place.

Cathy learns about her cousin

I ordered Cathy to be quiet and we fetched the pony ourselves, and the dogs, and started on our way home. Cathy could not understand the position of Hareton in that house, and she questioned me about him. At last I was forced to tell

20 her the true story, that Hareton was her cousin. She was very surprised, for she could not understand that one who looked, dressed, and spoke like a workman, could be her cousin. I smiled at her reaction to the news. But Hareton, in spite of his disadvantages, was a well built youth, and good looking

25 too. Mr Heathcliff had not treated him badly, physically, he had only prevented him from having the kind of education and upbringing that should have been his by right. He could not read or write. His faults were not corrected, nor any good example set for him in that place where Mr Heathcliff ruled.

14   Linton's New Home

A letter, edged in black, announced the day when my master would return. Isabella was dead. He wrote to me to tell me of that fact, and that he would be returning with his nephew Linton. He told me to make a room ready for the new arrival.

Catherine was full of joy at the idea of welcoming her 5 father back, and seeing her real cousin, as she called him. The evening of their expected arrival came. She made me walk with her down to the main gate to meet them. She seated herself on the grass beside the path, and tried to wait patiently, but she could not be still for a minute. At length her 10 waiting was over, we could hear a carriage coming up the road. As soon as she saw her father's face, looking from the window of the carriage, she cried out with happiness and stretched up her arms. He got out quickly, nearly as eager as she was. While they were greeting each other, I took a quick 15 look in the carriage to see Linton.

He was asleep in a corner, wrapped in a warm blanket, as if it had been winter. He was a pale, delicate, weak looking boy.

'Now, darling,' said Mr Linton to Cathy, 'your cousin is 20 not so strong nor as merry as you are. He has only just lost his mother, so don't expect him to play and run about with you immediately. Let him be quiet this evening.'

'Yes, yes, Papa,' answered Cathy. 'But I do want to see him, and he hasn't once looked out.' 25

The sleeper was wakened and lifted to the ground by his uncle.

'Linton, this is your cousin Cathy,' he said. 'Don't upset her by crying. Try to be cheerful now, the travelling is at an end.' 30

'Let me go to bed then,' answered the boy.

We all walked up to the house and went inside. I placed

Linton on a chair by the table. As soon as he sat down, he
began to cry. My master asked what was wrong.

'I can't sit on a chair,' sobbed the boy.

'Go and sit on the sofa, then, and Ellen shall bring you
5 some tea,' answered his uncle patiently.

Linton walked slowly over to the sofa, and lay down.
Cathy carried his tea over to him and sat by his side. She
stroked his hair, and kissed his cheek, and offered him tea in
the saucer, like a baby. This pleased him, for he was not
10 much better than one.

'Oh, he'll be all right,' said the master to me. 'He'll be all
right, if we can keep him. The company of a child of his own
age will put new life into him.'

'Yes, if we can keep him,' I thought to myself, full of fear,
15 thinking that there was little hope of that. How could that
weak child live at Wuthering Heights, between his father and
Hareton? What terrible company and teachers they would be!

Heathcliff asks for his son

Our fears were soon to come true, even earlier than I had
expected. I had just taken the children upstairs after tea, and
20 seen that Linton was asleep, when Joseph appeared at the
front door. He refused to speak to me, insisting that he was
ordered to talk to Mr Linton.

'Heathcliff has sent me for his son,' said the old man to
Linton, 'and I mustn't go back without him.'

25 Edgar Linton was silent for a minute, an expression of
great sadness on his face. But there was nothing to do but
hand over the child, for Heathcliff had a right to his own son.
However, Mr Linton was not going to wake the child from
his sleep.

30 'Tell Mr Heathcliff,' he answered calmly, 'that his son
shall come to Wuthering Heights tomorrow. He is in bed, and
too tired to travel further today.'

'No!' said Joseph. 'Heathcliff will not listen to that excuse.
He wants his lad immediately, and I must take him, or I shall
35 suffer.'

'You shall not tonight!' answered Mr Linton. 'Repeat to your master what I have said. Ellen, show him out!'

'Very well,' said Joseph. 'Tomorrow morning, he'll come himself.'

To prevent this from happening, Mr Linton told me to take   5
the boy to his new home early in the morning. He could go on Cathy's pony. He added, 'As we shall not be able to help him further in any way, good or bad, you must not tell my daughter where he has gone. Tell her his father sent for him suddenly, and he has had to leave us.'   10

Linton was astonished to be informed that he must get ready for some more travelling.

'My father!' he cried, not understanding. 'Mamma never told me I had a father. Why didn't mamma and he live to-gether, as other people do?'   15

I could not answer his questions, so I tried to interest him in the new place he was going to. He seemed quite interested in his surroundings, once we had started on our journey.

'Is Wuthering Heights as pleasant as Thrushcross Grange?' he asked, turning to take a last look into the valley.   20

'It is not surrounded by so many trees,' I replied, 'and is not quite as large. But you can see the countryside all around, and the air will be healthier for you.'

The boy was fully occupied with his own thoughts for the rest of the ride.   25

Linton meets his father

We arrived at Wuthering Heights at half past six. The family had just finished breakfast. The servant was clearing the table, Joseph stood next to his master's chair, telling him some-thing about a lame horse. Hareton was getting ready to go out into the fields.   30

'Hullo, Nelly!' cried Mr Heathcliff when he saw me. 'I was afraid I would have to come down and fetch my property myself. You've brought it, have you? Let's see what it's like.'

He got up and walked to the door. Hareton and Joseph followed, filled with curiosity. Poor Linton ran a frightened   35
eye over the three of them.

'Surely,' said Joseph, after a long hard look, 'Mr Edgar's changed the children round, and this is his daughter!'

Heathcliff, having stared his son into confusion, gave a scornful laugh.

5 'God! What a beauty! Have they fed it only on milk, Nelly? But that's worse than I expected, and the devil knows, I didn't expect much.'

I told the trembling and unhappy child to get down and enter. He did not quite understand the meaning of his father's 10 speech, or even if it was directed at him. He was not yet certain that the stern terrifying stranger was his father. He held on to me with growing fear, and hid his face on my shoulder and wept.

Heathcliff dragged him roughly to him.

15 'Do you know me?' he asked.

'No,' said Linton, with a look of fear.

'No! What a pity your mother never told you of me, so that you could learn to love me, as a son should love his father! She was a wicked woman to leave you in ignorance of 20 your father. Now don't look like that, nor go red, though it is something to see that you do not have white blood.'

'I hope you'll be kind to the boy, Mr Heathcliff,' I said, 'or you'll not keep him long. He's the only relative you have in the world, remember.'

25 'I'll be very kind to him, you needn't fear,' he said, laughing. 'Only no one else must be kind to him. And to begin my kindness, Joseph, bring the lad some breakfast. Hareton, you fool, get off to your work.

'Yes, Nelly,' he added when they had all gone, Linton and 30 Joseph into the kitchen, and Hareton to the fields. 'My son will be the next owner of the Grange, and I should not wish him to die for that reason. Besides, he's mine, and I want the triumph of seeing my child control their lands. I want my child to hire their children to work their fathers' land for 35 simple wages. That is the only thing that could ever make me accept this weak child into my care. I despise him for himself, and hate him for the memories he brings with him, but he's safe with me. I have a room upstairs for him, and I've employed a teacher to come three times a week to teach him. I've ordered Hareton to obey him.'

Cathy is upset that Linton has gone
We had a lot of trouble with Cathy that day. She was so upset when she learned that Linton had already left. Edgar   *5* himself was forced to quieten her by saying that Linton would come back soon. He added, however, 'If I can get him.' There were no hopes of that.

When I happened to meet the housekeeper of Wuthering Heights, when I went to the village of Gimmerton for shop-   *10* ping, I used to ask how the young master was. I learnt from her that his health continued to be weak, and that he was a difficult child to please. Mr Heathcliff seemed to like him less and less. Linton learnt his lessons or else lay in bed all day. For he was always getting colds and coughs, or pains of some   *15* sort.

I learnt that the complete lack of sympathy that Linton received from the rest of the household at the Heights made him become a selfish and disagreeable young man. He probably would have been so anyway. Mr Edgar thought about   *20* him often, I think. But he never saw him again after that first meeting. Linton very rarely went out anywhere.

15   Heathcliff's Plan

Time went on at the Grange, till Cathy reached her sixteenth birthday. We never celebrated this day, for it was also the day on which her mother died. Her father always spent the day alone in the library, and walked in the evening to Gimmerton
5 churchyard.

This 20th of March was a beautiful day. When her father had gone into the library, my young lady came down dressed for going out. She said that she had asked if she might go on the moors for a walk with me, and Mr Linton had given her
10 permission, provided that we didn't go too far.

Cathy meets Heathcliff at last

I put on my hat and we went out, having no worries in the world. Cathy ran in front of me like a young dog. She was a happy creature in those days. There were so many little hills and banks to climb that I soon began to tire. I told my com-
15 panion that we must stop and turn round to go home. I shouted to her, as she had gone a long way ahead of me, but she either did not hear my calls, or was taking no notice. I was forced to follow her, tired though I was. Finally she jumped down into a sheltered piece of land. As I caught up
20 with her, I saw that she had been stopped by two people, one of whom I was sure was Mr Heathcliff.

'Who are you?' I heard her ask Heathcliff. 'I've seen your companion before. Is he your son?'

'Miss Cathy,' I interrupted, 'we have been out three hours
25 instead of one. We really must go back.'

'No, that man is not my son,' answered Heathcliff, pushing me aside. 'But I have one, and you have seen him before, you know. Though your nurse is in a hurry to be gone, I think both you and she should rest for a while. Would you like to
30 come to my house? You'll be able to travel home more quick-

ly after you have rested, and you will get a kind welcome there.'

I whispered to Cathy that she must not accept his invitation.

'Why?' she said aloud. 'I'm tired of running, and the ground   *5*
is too wet to sit on. Let us go there, Ellen. Besides, he says I have seen his son. I expect he lives at the farm-house I visited before.'

She ran around the corner of the hill at full speed, Hareton running with her.   *10*

'Mr Heathcliff, it is very wrong,' I said. 'You know you mean no good by this. And she'll see Linton there, and she'll tell her father all about it when we return. And I shall be blamed for everything.'

'I want her to see Linton,' he answered. 'We'll soon per-   *15*
suade her to keep the visit a secret. My purpose is as honest as it could be – that two cousins may fall in love, and get married. I'm acting generously to your master. His young girl has no fortune, and if she agrees to my wishes, she will become joint future owner with Linton of her father's lands.'   *20*

'If Linton died,' I answered, 'and his life is quite uncertain, Catherine would get his lands.'

'No, she would not,' he said. 'The legal papers on this point do not say so. His property would go to me, his sister's husband. But to prevent unnecessary arguments I want my son   *25*
and his daughter to be married, and I am determined to make it happen.'

'I am determined that she will never come near your house again, especially in my care,' I replied. We reached the gate, where Cathy was waiting for us.   *30*

Cathy sees Linton for the second time

Heathcliff told me to be quiet, and hurried to open the door. Linton stood there near the fire. He had been out walking, for his hat was on, and he was calling to Joseph to bring him dry shoes. He had grown tall for his age, still just short of sixteen.   *35*

'Now, who is that?' asked Mr Heathcliff, turning to Cathy.

'Your son?' she said, having doubtfully looked from one to the other.

'Yes, yes, but is this the only time you have seen him? Think! You have a short memory.'

5   'Why, it is Linton!' cried Cathy, her face filling with joyful surprise.

'Is it really little Linton? He's taller than I am!'

The youth stepped forward, and Cathy kissed him. She had reached her full height, and her whole appearance 10 sparkled with health and good spirits. Linton's looks and movements were pale and limp by comparison. He was thin, but he looked quite pleasing.

'So, you are my uncle, then!' cried Cathy to Heathcliff, stretching up to give him a kiss to mark the occasion of dis-15 covering a new uncle.

'I thought I liked you, though you were angry at first. Why don't you visit the Grange with Linton? To live all these years such close neighbours, and never see each other, it is odd!'

'I visited it once or twice too often before you were born,' 20 he answered. 'If you have any kisses to spare, give them to Linton, they are wasted on me.'

'Naughty Ellen, to try and stop me from entering my uncle's home!' exclaimed Cathy. 'But I'll take this walk every morning in future. May I uncle?'

25   'Of course,' replied the uncle, 'but, now that I think of it, I'd better tell you. Your father does not care for me. We quarrelled at one time in our lives, and if you mention to him that you are coming here, he'll not let you come again.'

'Why did you quarrel?' she asked, upset at what he had 30 just said.

'He thought me too poor to marry his sister,' answered Heathcliff. 'Then he became even more angry when I did. His pride was hurt, and he'll never forgive me.'

'That's wrong!' said Cathy. 'But Linton and I have no share 35 in your quarrel. I'll not come here then, he shall come to the Grange.'

'It would be too far for me,' said her cousin. 'To walk four

miles would kill me. No, come here Miss Catherine, sometimes. Not every morning, but once or twice a week.'

Hareton
I saw the father give his son a look of scorn after those
words were spoken.

'I am afraid, Nelly, all my labour will be wasted,' Heath-   *5*
cliff muttered to me. 'She will discover what he is worth, and
send him to the devil. Now, if it had been Hareton! Twenty
times a day I wish Hareton was my son, in spite of how he
has fallen in the world. He is worth ten times as much as this
poor weak creature. We don't think he will even reach   *10*
twenty. Look at him, he's only thinking about his wet feet.
He never looks at the girl! Linton!'

'Yes, Father?'

'Don't you have anything to show your cousin, not even
a rabbit, or perhaps a bird's nest? Take her into the garden,   *15*
and into the stables to see your horse.'

'Wouldn't you rather sit here?' asked Linton, speaking to
Cathy in a reluctant tone.

'I don't mind,' she replied, looking towards the door with
an expression on her face which showed clearly that she   *20*
would rather be outside being active.

He stayed in his chair, and leant his hands towards the fire.
Heathcliff went into the yard, calling for Hareton. Presently
the two entered. Cathy whispered in Heathcliff's ear, and he
laughed. Hareton looked angry. I saw that he was easily upset *25*
if he thought someone was making fun of him.

But Hareton's frown disappeared when Heathcliff added,
'You'll be the favourite among us, Hareton! She said something very nice about you. You go with her around the farm,
and behave like a gentleman, don't forget! Don't use any bad   *30*
words, and take your hands out of your pockets. Look after
her nicely.'

He watched the pair of them walk past the window.

'I've made sure he won't say a word,' laughed Heathcliff.
'He'll not even dare to say one word!'   *35*

He continued, 'I get a real pleasure from Hareton. He has completely satisfied what I hoped for. If he had been born a fool, I would not be able to enjoy this half as much. But he's no fool, and I can sympathize with all his feelings, having
5 felt them myself. I know what he suffers now, for instance, exactly. It is merely the beginning of what he shall suffer in the future, though. And he'll never be able to drag himself up from his roughness and ignorance. I've trapped him here far more tightly than his horrible father managed to trap me, and
10 lower too, for Hareton takes pride in his animal-like behaviour. Don't you think that Hindley would be proud of his son if he could see him, almost as proud of him as I am of mine? But there's the difference. Mine has nothing of value about him, yet I shall make him do quite well, and go quite
15 far. Hindley's son had first-class qualities, and they are lost, made worse than useless. And the best of it is, Hareton is very fond of me!'

Heathcliff laughed wickedly at this. Then he noticed his son's restless looks towards the window.
20 'Get up! You idle boy!' he exclaimed. 'Go and join them.'

Linton got up slowly and left the fire. As he stepped out, I heard Cathy ask the still silent Hareton what was the meaning of the words over the door.

'It's some stupid writing,' he answered. 'I cannot read it.'
25 'Can't read it!' cried Catherine.

Linton laughed. 'He doesn't know how to read,' he said. 'You see now, Hareton, the result of taking no notice of books and learning.'

'Where the devil is the use of it?' scorned Hareton.
30 'Where is the use of the devil in that sentence?' laughed Linton nastily. 'Father told you not to use any bad words, and you can't open your mouth without one coming out. Do try to behave like a gentleman.'

'If you looked more like a lad than a girl, I'd fight you
35 right now, you pitiful creature,' replied the angry boy. He knew he had been insulted, and did not know what to do about it.

Edgar forbids Cathy to go to the Heights

We stayed until after lunch, I could not persuade Miss Cathy to come away before. Happily my master had not left his library, and he remained ignorant of our long absence. But next day the visit was revealed. Miss Cathy was determined to tell her father that he was wrong to keep such old *5* hatred alive. I was not sorry, that everything was now out in the open. I did not like having secrets from the master. Cathy gave a truthful account of our trip. She could not understand her father's feelings towards Heathcliff.

'He was very pleasant, father,' she said, 'and he is willing to *10* let Linton and me be friends.'

But it was no good. Nothing could persuade Mr Linton to agree to his daughter's wish to go to Wuthering Heights again.

Poor Miss Cathy, she did not know of bad deeds, except her own slight acts of disobedience, for which she was sorry *15* on the same day that she had done them. She was amazed, therefore, by the kind of anger and hatred that could continue for years. She appeared deeply shocked by this new view on human nature, and in the evening I found her crying on her knees by her bed. *20*

'I'm not crying for myself, Nelly,' she said, 'but for Linton. Because of an argument two men had, over sixteen years ago, Linton will not see me tomorrow as he expected, and he'll be so disappointed. He'll wait for me, and I shan't come.'

'Nonsense!' I said. 'Do you imagine that he has thought of *25* you as you have of him? He has Hareton for a companion. And no one would cry about losing a relation that they had only seen twice, on two afternoons. Linton will realize what has happened, and bother himself no more about it.'

'But can't I just write a note to tell him why I cannot *30* come?' she asked. 'And just send those books I promised to lend him.'

'No, you may not!' I replied firmly.

'But how can one little note – ' she started again.

'Be quiet!' I said. 'And go to bed. I don't want to hear any *35* more about it.'

She gave me such a naughty look that I would not kiss her

good-night. I went out, but feeling a little guilty, I returned
to give her my normal good-night kiss. I returned softly, and
there was Cathy, standing at the table with a piece of paper in
front of her and a pencil in her hand, which she guiltily
5 slipped out of sight.

'You'll get no one to take that, Cathy,' I said, 'if you do
write it. Now, I shall put out your candle.'

Cathy's secret letters

I put out the flame, kissed her, and left the room again.
She locked the door behind me. The letter was finished, and
10 sent by the boy from the village who delivers the milk. But
I did not learn of that till some time afterwards.

Weeks passed, and my suspicions were finally aroused by
Cathy's secret, hidden activities with a drawer in a cupboard
in the library. One night, as soon as she and my master were
15 safe upstairs in their beds, I easily found a key that would fit
in the lock of the drawer. I emptied the contents into my
apron and took them up to my own room to examine. There
were many notes from Linton Heathcliff, answers to ones
sent by her. I examined them all, and found the later ones to
20 be love letters. In the morning, I watched in the kitchen, and
saw a boy arrive. While the maid took some milk from his
can, Cathy pushed a note into his pocket, and at the same
time, withdrew one from it as well. As the boy walked away
I stopped him, and took the letter Cathy had put in his
25 pocket.

We had an argument later, when Cathy found I had taken
all her letters.

'I didn't mean to start writing,' she sobbed. 'I didn't think
of loving him till —.'

30 'Loving!' I said scornfully. 'I might just as well talk of
loving the man who comes once a year to buy our apples.
Loving indeed! You can hardly have seen him for more than
four hours altogether in the two times that you have seen
him!'

35 She sobbed and cried when I said I must show the letters

to her father, until at last I agreed to burn them, providing she promised to write no more. She did so, and I started to burn the letters, making sure that none remained. Next morning I answered Linton's last note with a note of my own:

'Master Linton Heathcliff is requested to send no more   5 notes to Miss Linton, as she will no longer accept them.'

From that time onwards, the milk-boy came with empty pockets.

16   Linton Grows Weaker

The summer and early autumn of 1799 were coming to an end. I was out walking with Cathy. It was a fresh damp October afternoon, and I discovered that my little mistress was crying.

5   'You mustn't cry because your father has a cold and cannot come out,' I said. 'Be thankful it is not something worse.'

'Oh, it will be something worse!' she said, making no attempt to control her tears. 'And what shall I do when you and Papa leave me?'

10   'No one can tell whether you might not even die before us,' I replied. 'It's wrong to think of such things. We'll hope there are years and years to come before any of us go. Your father is young, and I am strong, and only just forty-five. My mother lived till eighty.'

15   'But Aunt Isabella was younger than Papa,' she remarked.

'Aunt Isabella did not have you and me to nurse her,' I replied. 'All you need to do is look after your father, and cheer him by letting him see that you are cheerful. Avoid causing worry on any subject. Don't forget that, Cathy.'

20   'I'll never do anything, nor say anything that could upset him. I love him better than myself, Ellen.'

As we talked, we approached a door in the wall that opened on to the road. My young lady climbed up and seated herself on top of the wall. In stretching up to reach for some flowers
25   on a wild rose tree, her hat fell off. As the door was locked, she had to climb down off the wall to get it. The hat had fallen on the road side of the wall, and getting up again from that side was not easy. The stones of the wall were smooth and there were no bushes or cracks in the stones that could
30   help someone climbing in. I, like a fool, had not thought of this when Cathy had told me she must climb down to get her hat. She called to me from the other side, 'Ellen, you'll have

to go and find the key to the gate in the wall that I can see just near here. Otherwise I'll have to run all the way round to the main gate, which is a long way. I cannot get up again from this side.'

Heathcliff again

5   I was about to hurry back to get the key, when an approaching sound stopped me. It was a horse coming towards us.

'Who is that?' I whispered to Cathy.

'Hello, Miss Linton!' cried a deep voice. 'I'm glad to meet
10 you. Don't be in a hurry to try and enter, for I have a question to ask you, and I want an answer.'

'I shan't speak to you, Mr Heathcliff,' answered Cathy.

'Two or three months ago,' said Heathcliff, 'you used to write to Linton. I suppose you grew tired of this amusement
15 and stopped, didn't you? Well you have caused Linton to become very unhappy. I speak the truth when I say he's dying because of you. He's breaking his heart. He is getting worse daily, and he'll be dead and buried before next summer, unless you do something about it.'

20   'How can you lie like that to the poor child?' I called from the other side of the wall, for I could hear quite clearly what was being said. 'Please go away!'

'I did not realize that there was anyone else here,' muttered Heathcliff. 'Dear Nelly, I like you, but I don't want you
25 to interfere now. Catherine, my girl, I shall not be at home all this week, so why don't you go over to Wuthering Heights yourself, and see if I have spoken the truth or not! I swear he's going to his grave, and only you can save him!'

I could bear it no longer, so I picked up a stone and broke
30 the lock. Then I opened it quickly and came out on the other side. Heathcliff saw me at once.

'Nelly,' he said, 'if you won't let her go, you can walk over yourself, and tell her what you find. I shall not be back there until this time next week.'

35   'Come in,' I said, taking Cathy by the arm. She pulled against me, for she did not want to go yet.

'Miss Catherine, let me tell you that I have very little patience with Linton, and Hareton and Joseph have less. He lives with hard, unfriendly people. He needs kindness and love, so a kind word from you would be his best medicine. Don't listen to Nelly's words, but try to see him. Surely your father wouldn't mind you visiting your cousin.' 5

Poor Cathy was very troubled by Heathcliff's words, and she did not speak to me all the way back to the house.

My master had already gone to his room to rest before we came in, so Cathy and I had tea alone together. She cried all through it. I told her that Mr Heathcliff was probably lying about his son. But nothing I said could really persuade her that what he had told her was not true. 10

'You may be right, Ellen,' she answered, 'but I cannot be sure. I will not feel happy about the matter till I know for myself. And I must tell Linton that it is not my fault that I no longer write to him.' 15

Ellen and Cathy visit Linton

I could not bear to see her so worried and sad, so I gave in. I said that we would both go and find out the truth for ourselves tomorrow. I was hoping that Linton himself might prove that his father had not told the truth. So, the next day I was on the road to Wuthering Heights, walking by the side of my mistress on her pony. We entered the farmhouse through the kitchen door. Joseph was sitting alone beside a roaring fire, drinking a cup of tea and smoking a pipe. We heard Linton's voice coming from inside another room, so we went through to it. 20

'Is that you, Miss Linton?' he said, raising his head. 'No, don't kiss me, it takes my breath away. Papa said you would come. Will you shut the door, please? You left it open. The servants won't bring me any more wood for the fire, and it's so cold in here.' 25 30

I went out myself, and fetched some wood. The boy had a bad cough and looked feverish and ill.

'Well, Linton,' asked Cathy softly, 'are you glad to see me? Can I do you any good?' 35

'Why didn't you come before?' he asked. 'You should have come instead of writing. I got very tired writing those long letters. I wonder where the servant is. I want a drink. Her name is Zillah, will you please call her.' He looked at me.

5   'Don't worry,' said Cathy. She had seen a jug of water on a table, and she brought it over to Linton.

'Does your father look after you well?' I asked.

'I suppose you could say that, at least he makes the servants look after me.'

10   Having swallowed some water, Linton became a little more friendly.

'I am glad to see you,' he said. 'It's something new to hear your voice. But I have been annoyed because you wouldn't come before. Papa said that you didn't like me. You do, don't

15 you, Miss — .'

'I wish you would say Catherine, or Cathy,' interrupted my young lady. 'Like you? Of course! Next to papa and Ellen, I love you better than anyone else I know. I don't love Mr Heathcliff, though, and I dare not come when he returns.

20 Where has he gone?'

'Since the shooting season started he goes up on the moors for days at a time. Do say you will come and spend an hour or two with me when he isn't here.'

'Yes,' said Cathy, stroking his long soft hair. 'Pretty Lin-

25 ton! I wish you were my brother.'

'And then you would like me as much as your father?' said Linton happily. 'But Papa says you would love me better than him, and everyone else if you were my wife, so I'd rather you were that.'

30   This talk went on for some time, until they eventually started quarrelling about their fathers. I thought it was time to go, and I told Cathy so.

'Must I go?' she asked unhappily. 'Do you want me to go, Linton?'

35   'Leave me alone now,' he said 'I've had enough of your talking for today, it makes me tired. But please come tomorrow, Catherine. Will you come tomorrow?'

'No,' I answered, 'nor the next day either.' Catherine, however, bent down and whispered in his ear. He looked much
happier after that, so I realized that she must have given him
a different answer from mine.

'I'll be careful,' I said. 'I'll have that broken lock on the   *5*
gate mended, and you cannot escape anywhere else.'

'I can get over the wall,' she said laughing. 'The Grange is
not a prison, Ellen, and you cannot treat me like a prisoner.
Besides, I'm almost seventeen. I'm a woman.'

With those words, we left Linton and returned home.   *10*

Ellen dislikes Linton

'Don't you like Linton, Ellen?' asked Cathy.

'Like him!' I exclaimed. 'He's the most bad-tempered,
weak person that ever lived. Happily, as Mr Heathcliff said,
he'll not live to be twenty. Indeed, I doubt if he'll live to see
the spring. And it'll be a small loss to his family when he   *15*
goes. I'm glad you have no chance of having him for a hus-
band, Miss Catherine.'

My companion looked very serious and upset that I had
spoken so harshly of Linton.

'He's a pretty thing when he's good. I'd be so good to him   *20*
if he were mine. We should never quarrel, should we, after
we got used to each other?' she asked, as though thinking
aloud.

'Well,' I said, 'let's not bother about young Linton any
more, Miss. I warn you, and I shall keep my promise, if you   *25*
attempt to go to Wuthering Heights again, with or without
me, I shall inform Mr Linton. And, unless he lets you go, you
will not see your cousin again.'

Ellen is ill

We reached home before dinner-time. As soon as I could, I
changed my wet shoes. It had been cold and wet, walking to
and from Wuthering Heights. I was afraid I might have caught   *30*
a cold, and the next day my fears were confirmed and I had
to go to bed. I did not recover from that day for three weeks.

I had to stay in bed all that time, and could do none of my normal duties, something that had never happened to me before, and never since.

My little mistress behaved like an angel towards me, always coming in to cheer me up and get anything that I wanted. As soon as Cathy left her father in his room, where he was also ill, she came to my bedside. Her day was divided between us. She was the fondest nurse that I have ever seen. But the master liked to be left alone early, and I usually needed nothing after six o'clock, thus the evenings were her own. Poor thing! I never bothered to think what she might do to amuse herself after tea. Frequently, when she looked in to say good-night, I noticed a fresh colour in her cheeks. But instead of thinking that the colour came from a cold ride across the moors, I thought that she had got her rosy cheeks from sitting in front of a hot fire inside.

17 Imprisoned in Wuthering Heights

At the end of three weeks, I was able to leave my room and move about the house. On the first occasion when I sat up in the evening, I asked Cathy to read to me, because my eyes were weak. She made all kinds of excuses so that she would not have to do it. Finally, she complained that she had a *5* headache, and she left me. I thought her behaviour odd, and, after a while, decided to ask her to come and lie on the sofa, instead of lying in her room in the dark. I could find Cathy nowhere, neither upstairs, nor downstairs.

The moon was shining brightly. A little snow covered the *10* ground, and I thought that she might have gone out in the garden for a walk. Then I saw one of the stable lads leading Cathy's pony, and she was walking next to them. She entered the sitting room through one of the glass doors. I suddenly moved out from where I had been watching. She was so sur- *15* prised to see me that she could not move.

Cathy's secret visits

'My dear Miss Catherine,' I began, 'where have you been?'

She burst into tears, ran to me and threw her arms round my neck.

'Well, Ellen, promise not to be angry, and you shall know *20* the truth. I hate to hide it.'

We sat down in the window-seat.

'I've been to Wuthering Heights, Ellen, and I've not missed a day since you fell ill. I gave one of the stable lads, who is fond of reading, books and pictures so that he would get my *25* pony ready every evening and put her back in the stable when I returned. You mustn't scold him, Ellen. It wasn't his fault. I usually got to the Heights by half-past six, and stayed till half past eight. Then I galloped home. I did not go to amuse myself. I often felt terrible about what I was doing. *30*

'On my second visit, Linton seemed to be much happier.
Joseph and Hareton were out, and Zillah, their housekeeper,
brought me some warm wine and some biscuits. Linton and
I talked and laughed merrily. Once, though, we came close to
5 quarrelling. We were playing a game, and I was winning all the
time, and he got very angry. And once there was a quarrel
between Hareton and Linton. Somehow Linton got hurt.
Blood gushed from his mouth. I ran into the yard, sick with
terror, and called for Zillah. When I got back to see how Lin-
10 ton was, he would neither speak to me, nor look at me, Ellen.
He has such a bad temper. When he did open his mouth, he
lied, and said that I had caused all the trouble, and that Hareton was not to blame! I got up and went home, I was so
angry. But, on my next visit we became friends again.
15 'About three times, I think, we were happy and carefree,
as we were that first visit. But the rest of my visits were unpleasant, because he was nasty, or he was feeling ill. Mr
Heathcliff avoids me on purpose, I think he knows that I
wouldn't have gone if he had always been around. Now,
20 Ellen, you have heard everything.'

I told the whole story to Mr Linton the next morning.
Catherine was told that her secret visits must end. She cried
in vain, and asked her father to have pity on Linton. She only
got a promise that he would write and give Linton permission
25 to come to the Grange.

Linton did not come, of course. I had to explain to the
master that it was not because he did not want to, but that
he was not strong enough.

The spring of 1800 was coming, but my master did not
30 become any stronger, though he started to walk around with
his daughter again. She thought this was a sign that he was
getting better, but I thought otherwise. On her seventeenth
birthday he was not able to visit his wife's grave. He was no
longer strong enough.

35 Mr Linton wrote again to his nephew, asking him to visit
the Grange. I think he felt that when he died he should not
leave Cathy alone in the world, so he decided to forget his

quarrel with Heathcliff for the good of his daughter. It was
Linton she wanted to see after all, not Heathcliff. And when
I told him that Linton was not at all like his father, he felt
happier. But again Linton could not come because he was not
strong enough. So in the end, Catherine was allowed to visit   *5*
Linton once a week, but not at Wuthering Heights. A meeting
place nearby, not too far for Linton, was arranged.

The first time we set out to join Cathy's cousin, it was a
hot, unpleasant day. When we found Linton he looked very
pale. Cathy looked at him with grief and astonishment.   *10*

'I'm tired,' he said. 'It's too hot for walking. And in the
morning I often feel sick.'

'I think,' said Cathy, 'that you'd be more comfortable at
home than sitting here.'

Indeed Linton looked terrible, and soon, in spite of Cathy's   *15*
company, fell asleep. By the time he had woken up, it was
time for us to go. We agreed to meet again on the following
Thursday.

Edgar Linton is very ill

But in the next seven days, there was a rapid change in
Edgar Linton's health. He was really very ill now, and Cathy   *20*
hated the thought of the death of her beloved father, which
she knew she must soon face. By the time the next Thursday
had arrived, poor Cathy could not decide whether to stay
with her father or go to see Linton. In the end we went, in
the afternoon.   *25*

When we found Linton this time, he looked not ill, but
terrified. He told Cathy that she must not leave him, or, he
said, he would be killed. My young lady, seeing how real his
terror was, grew very worried and upset.

'My father threatened me,' said the boy, 'and I fear him.'   *30*

He wept wildly, holding on to Cathy with all his poor
strength. I couldn't understand what was going on. Then I
looked up and saw Heathcliff.

'How are you Nelly, and all those at the Grange? They say,'
he added, in a lower tone, 'that Edgar Linton is dying.'   *35*

'It is true,' I answered, 'and it will be a sad thing for all of us.'

'How long will he last? That boy of mine seems determined to die first, and that does not suit my purpose. I would like his uncle to be quick and go before him. Hello, Miss Linton, how is my boy?' asked Heathcliff of Cathy.

'He looks terrible. I think he should be in bed, under the care of a doctor.'

'Get up, Linton, get up!' Heathcliff shouted, looking with hate at his son.

Linton made several efforts to obey, but he wasn't strong enough. He fell back again.

'Leave me alone or I shall faint,' he whispered to his father. 'Stay near me Catherine, give me your hand.'

'Be so kind, Miss Linton,' said Heathcliff, 'to walk home with him. He cannot bear it if I touch him.'

'Linton, dear!' whispered Catherine, 'I can't go to Wuthering Heights with you. Papa has forbidden it. Your father won't harm you. Why are you so afraid?'

'I am not to return to that house without you!'

Heathcliff locks the door

However much I argued, I could not stop her going back with him. I would not enter when we reached the door. Cathy walked in, and I waited outside till she would be ready to join me. But Mr Heathcliff pushed me forward through the door, saying, 'My house is not full of disease, Nelly. Sit down and allow me to shut the door.'

He shut it, and locked it too. I looked up with sudden fear.

'I'm not afraid of you!' exclaimed Cathy, who had just seen Heathcliff's actions. 'Give me that key.'

'You be careful, Catherine Linton,' said Heathcliff, 'or I'll hit you.'

Ignoring this warning, she grabbed at his hand that held the key, scratching and biting in trying to get it. She did not see his face, but I did. It was full of hate. He opened his hand, letting her get the key, but then he gave her two terrible blows across the head. I rushed at him, furious.

'You madman,' I shouted, grabbing at him. But I was not strong enough. With one push he sent me falling to the ground, beaten.

He turned to the poor, trembling Cathy. 'Go to Linton, now,' he said, but she ran to comfort and find comfort with me.

Heathcliff informed us he was going outside for a while, and told us to have some tea while we waited.

Our first thought, on his departure, was to try to get out. We tried the kitchen door, but that was locked from the outside, and the windows were too small to get through, even for Cathy with her slim figure.

'Master Linton,' I cried, 'you know what your father intends to do, and you shall tell us, or I'll hit you, like that devil of a man just hit Cathy.'

'Yes, Linton, you must tell us,' said Cathy.

'Give me some tea, I'm thirsty,' was all he said.

I felt disgusted by the boy's behaviour. Now that he was no longer afraid for himself, he didn't care about anyone else. I guessed that he had done what he had been told to do, to get us into the house, and therefore did not have any immediate fears.

'Papa wants us to get married,' he continued, after drinking his tea, 'and he's afraid that I shall die if we wait any longer. We are to be married in the morning. You are to stay here tonight. If you do as he wishes, you shall return home soon, and take me with you.'

'Stay here all night? No!' she said. 'Ellen, I'll burn that door down if I have to, to get out.'

And she would have started it immediately, but Linton stopped her, fearing for himself again.

'You must marry me, and save me, Catherine, you must!' He was terrified. 'You must obey my father,' he kept saying.

'I must obey my own,' she replied. 'Be quiet! You're in no danger. But if you try and stop me —.'

At that moment Heathcliff came back in. He looked around at us all. He obviously could bear the sight of his son no longer, so he sent him to bed.

Cathy is a prisoner until she marries Linton

After Linton had gone upstairs Cathy tried to persuade Heathcliff to let her return home to see her father.

'I promise to marry Linton,' she said. 'Just let me go, father will be so worried and miserable if he thinks I am lost.'

5   'Miss Linton, I shall enjoy myself very much by thinking your father will be miserable. As to your promise to marry Linton, I shall make sure that you keep it. For you shall not leave this house until that event happens!'

'Send Ellen, then, to let Papa know that I am safe!' ex-
10 claimed Cathy, crying.

'Weep as much as you like, it will be your main amusement from now on,' said the monster.

He had sent away all the rest of the household, so we were told to sleep in the housekeeper's room. I whispered to my
15 companion to obey. We might be able to escape through a window there. The window, unfortunately, was like the windows downstairs — it was too narrow.

Neither of us could sleep that night. We waited anxiously for morning, hoping that the new day might bring new hope.

20 At seven o'clock, Heathcliff came up and demanded to speak to Cathy. She ran to the door immediately, and he opened it, pulling her out of the room in one quick movement. I rose to follow, but he shut the door in my face and locked it again.

25 I remained in that room for four days and five nights, seeing no one but Hareton, who brought me some food. He would say nothing, nor help me in any way other than bringing the food and so preventing me from starving.

18 The Death of Edgar Linton

Ellen escapes

On the fifth afternoon, Zillah came up.

She knew nothing of what had happened, for she had been away. On her return, Heathcliff had only told her that he had rescued me from the moors where I had been lost.

'He gave me the key to the room, saying that you had been   *5* feverish and needed to be locked up, but that you were all right now and could return home to the Grange. He also said that your young lady would soon follow, and be in time to attend Mr Linton's funeral.'

'Mr Edgar is not dead?' I cried.   *10*

'No, not yet,' she answered. 'I met the doctor on the way here, and he thinks Mr Linton may last another day.'

I hastily grabbed my hat and coat and hurried downstairs, for I was eager to be free. The front door was open, and the place was filled with sunshine, but there was no sign of   *15* Catherine. Linton lay on the sofa.

'Where is Miss Catherine?' I asked.

'She's locked in a room upstairs,' he replied, 'and she's not allowed to leave yet.'

'Don't be so stupid,' I exclaimed. 'Show me where she is   *20* at once.'

'I will not! Papa told me to be firm with Catherine, now she's my wife. Papa says she hates me and only wants me to die so that she can have all my money.'

He would not tell me which room my poor Cathy was in,   *25* nor where he had hidden the key anyway. Neither Zillah nor Hareton knew either, so in the end I thought it would be better to leave alone and to come back, with some help, to rescue her as soon as I could.

The other servants at the Grange, when they saw me, were   *30* amazed and joyful. Everyone thought Cathy and I had been

lost on the moors. I found Mr Edgar very changed, even in
the few days I had been away. He lay on his bed, sad and
quiet, waiting for his death. He thought of Catherine, for he
whispered her name.

5   'Cathy is coming, dear master,' I said. 'She is alive and
well.' I told him all that had happened to us, and asked permission to send four men up to the Heights to rescue Miss
Cathy. He agreed to this immediately, of course, and I wasted
no time in asking the men to go. They were gone a long time,
10   and when they returned, they had no Cathy with them.

I had gone downstairs at three o'clock, when a sharp knock
at the front door made me jump. It was my own dear mistress. She had escaped herself, before the Grange men had
arrived! She was so pleased to see me, and fell into my arms,
15   sobbing.

Edgar Linton dies

Then I took her gently up to her father's room. I could not
bear to be with them at this last meeting between father and
daughter, so I stood outside the door for a long time before
I went in. Catherine's despair was as silent as her father's joy.

20   He died happily. Kissing her cheek, he whispered, 'I'm
going to join my wife, and you, darling child, will join us in
your own time,' and he never moved nor spoke again.

Catherine cried until she could cry no longer. Then she sat
there, next to her father, until the sun rose. She wanted to
25   stay there, dry-eyed and staring, but I insisted that she came
downstairs and had something to eat.

She told me how she had escaped. She had become so upset that she had terrified Linton into taking the risk of freeing
her. She was then able to creep out of the house before dawn.
30   We learned later how Heathcliff had his revenge for the disobedience of his son.

Heathcliff is the master of Thrushcross Grange

The evening after the funeral, my young lady and I were
seated in the library, when Heathcliff entered. He was legally
the master now and he acted as the master when he walked

into that house without knocking. It was the same room that
he had entered eighteen years before, as a guest of the dead
master and mistress. The same moon shone through the window, and the same autumn scenery lay outside. We had not
yet lit the candles, but one could still see quite clearly, even   5
the pictures on the wall. There were two especially good ones.
One, the head of Mrs Linton, and the other a graceful one of
her husband.

Heathcliff saw the one of Mrs Linton immediately, and
without any hesitation, he ordered me to have it sent over to   10
Wuthering Heights the next day.

Then he turned to Cathy, who had risen and was about to
leave the room.

'Stop!' he said. 'I've come to take you home, and I hope
you will be a dutiful daughter, and not encourage my son to   15
any more disobedience.'

'Why not let Cathy live here,' I asked, 'and send Linton to
her? You hate them both, so you won't miss them.'

He answered that he intended to rent the Grange, and that
he expected me to stay and be housekeeper to his new   20
tenants*. He would not let me go with my mistress to the
Heights.

'Good-bye Ellen,' whispered my dear Catherine. 'Come
and see me often, don't forget.'

'You will do no such thing!' said Heathcliff. 'When I want   25
to speak to you, I'll come here. I don't want you interfering
at the Heights.'

Linton is dead
Some time later I met Zillah in the village. She did not like
my Cathy.

'Mrs Heathcliff began to bother me,' she said, 'about her   30
husband, who was very ill. I said I had enough to do with my
own jobs. Mr Heathcliff had told me that looking after Linton was her job, not mine. I was not going to disobey the
master, though I thought it wrong that Dr Kennedy was not
sent for.   35

*tenant, person who lives in a house and pays rent to the owner.

'Then one evening, she came rushing into my room, and terrified me by saying, "Tell Mr Heathcliff that his son is dying. Get up at once and tell him."

'I rushed to find the master and told him exactly what she
5 had said. We both ran to Linton's room. Mrs Heathcliff was seated by the bedside with her hands folded on her knees. Her father-in-law went up and touched Linton. He was dead.

' "Now, Catherine," he said, "how do you feel?"

' "He's beyond your reach now, so you only have me left
10 to deal with," she answered.

' "Yes indeed," Heathcliff told her, and then he showed her Linton's will. Linton had left everything that he owned to his father. He had been forced to do it just after he had helped Cathy to escape from the Heights that day her father
15 had died. Catherine has nothing. She is now totally dependent on her father-in-law.'

It was thus, through Zillah, that I learnt of my Cathy's brief, unhappy married life. She now had no friends in the world but me.

19   Cathy and Hareton

Not long after I heard of Linton Heathcliff's death, a messenger appeared at Thrushcross Grange, ordering me to go to the Heights. I obeyed joyfully, for Cathy's sake. Mr Heathcliff did not explain his reasons for changing his mind about my coming. He only told me he wanted me, and he was tired of   *5* seeing Catherine working about the house all day. He had told Zillah she was no longer needed, once Linton had gone.

Cathy was very pleased to see me. Little by little I managed to bring over all her favourite books and other articles, that she had been forced to leave at the Grange before.   *10*

She was happy at first, with me there. But it was not long before she became bored and restless. She was not allowed to go out beyond the garden. She complained of loneliness, for I was forced to leave her alone quite often, in order to do my work in the house.   *15*

Cathy becomes friendly with Hareton

After a while, she began to take more interest in Hareton. She had not liked him at all before because he had been rude and unfriendly and a loyal servant of Heathcliff's.

'I know why Hareton never speaks when I am in the kitchen,' she exclaimed once. 'He is afraid I shall laugh at   *20* him. Ellen, what do you think? He began to teach himself to read once, and because I laughed, he burned his books and stopped. Wasn't that stupid?'

'Weren't you naughty?' I said. 'Answer me that.'

'Perhaps I was,' she said. 'I will try to be kinder.'   *25*

She left a book on the table, and hoped that he would take it. At first Hareton would have nothing to do with her, because he was still suspicious of her intentions. However she continued trying, and after a time they became friends.

One day I was ironing in the kitchen, and I watched them   *30* from time to time. I saw two happy faces bent over a book, and I did not doubt that they were both happy with each other.

'Come Catherine,' I said at last, 'we must go to bed. I've done my ironing. Are you ready?'

'Hareton,' she answered, rising unwillingly, 'I'll leave this book near the chimney, and I'll bring some more tomorrow.'

Smiling as she passed Hareton, she went singing upstairs. I think she was happier then than she ever had been under that roof before, except perhaps, during her earliest visits to Linton.

The next morning, Cathy went downstairs before me. She was out in the garden, where she had seen Hareton working. When I went out to tell them that breakfast was ready, I saw that she had persuaded him to clear a large space of ground which had contained fruit bushes. They were busy planning together what they would plant in their new flowerbed.

I was terrified at what they had done in the brief half hour that they had been out there together. The fruit bushes were Joseph's pride and joy, and she had just decided to put a flowerbed in the middle of them!

'There! That will be shown to the master,' I exclaimed, 'as soon as it is discovered. And what excuse can you give for doing such a thing? We shall all be punished for this, I'm sure. Mr Hareton I'm surprised at you, doing what she asks like that!'

'I'd forgotten they were Joseph's,' answered Hareton, 'but I'll tell him that it was my idea.'

We always ate our meals with Mr Heathcliff. Catherine usually sat near me, but today she was next to Hareton. I saw that she would be no more careful to hide her new friendship from Heathcliff than she had bothered to hide her dislike before.

'Now, you be careful not to take too much notice of your cousin,' I whispered to her. 'It will certainly annoy Mr Heathcliff, and he'll be angry with you both.'

'I'm not going to,' she answered.

But the next moment she had moved over to him, and was sticking little flowers in his food.

He dared not speak to her there, he hardly dared look. But he could not help laughing at her tricks. Mr Heathcliff looked up in surprise and saw what was going on.

'It's a good thing you are out of my reach,' he exclaimed to Cathy. 'Why are you staring at me with those eyes? Down with them! I thought I had cured you of laughing.'

'It was me,' muttered Hareton.

'What did you say?' demanded the master. Hareton looked at his plate, and did not repeat his confession. Heathcliff looked at him for a while, and then silently continued to eat.

Joseph wants to leave

We had nearly finished when Joseph appeared at the door. He showed, by the look of anger on his face, that he had found out what had happened to his precious bushes.

'I want to leave,' he announced. 'I had intended to die here, where I have served sixty years. I thought I would take my books up to my room, and let them have the kitchen to themselves. Even that was difficult to do, for I loved sitting down here by the fire in the evenings. But I thought I could bear that. But now she's taken my garden from me, and that, master, I cannot bear.'

'Now, now,' said Heathcliff, 'stop it! What is the matter? I'll not interfere in any quarrels between you and Nelly.'

'It's not Nelly,' answered Joseph. 'It's that terrible girl. She's made our lad fall in love with her. He's forgotten all that I've done for him, and torn up a whole row of the best fruit bushes in the garden!'

'Is the fool drunk?' asked Heathcliff. 'Hareton, what have you done?'

'I've pulled up two or three bushes,' replied the young man.

'We wanted to plant some flowers there,' cried Cathy. 'I'm the person to blame.'

'And who gave you permission to do such a thing?' asked her father-in-law, very surprised.

'You shouldn't mind me having a few yards of earth for flowers,' she replied. 'You have taken all the land that was rightfully mine.'

'Your land, you witch! You never had any! It was your
5   father's and then your husband's!'

'And my money,' she continued, returning his angry stare.

'Silence!' he shouted. 'Get out of here!'

'And Hareton's land, and his money,' continued the stupid thing. 'Hareton and I are friends now, and I shall tell him all
10   about you.'

The master grew pale and rose from his chair, looking at her with hate in his eyes. He was about to strike her. He had his hand in her hair. Hareton tried to free her, begging him not to hurt her. Heathcliff's black eyes flashed. He seemed
15   ready to tear Cathy to pieces. I was terrified, when suddenly his fingers relaxed. He looked at her face, then he put his hand over her eyes, so that he could no longer see them. Then he seemed to struggle with himself. He turned back to Cathy, and said with forced calmness, 'You must learn to avoid
20   making me so angry, or one day I will really murder you! Get out of my sight! And as for Hareton, if I find him listening to you, I'll send him from here immediately. Your love will make him a beggar. I'll see to that. Nelly, take her out of here. And leave me, all of you!'

25   I led my young lady out, and we spent a miserable day around the house until it was time for dinner. That was a silent, unhappy meal, with nobody speaking. Heathcliff went out immediately afterwards.

The two new friends sat there by the fire during his ab-
30   sence. Hareton refused to allow his cousin to tell him of what had happened to his father through Heathcliff's behaviour. Catherine got rather angry at this, until Hareton found just the right way to make her quiet. He asked her how she would like it if he spoke badly of her father. It was then that she
35   realized that Hareton looked upon Heathcliff as his father, and that she had no right to try and destroy his feelings.

When this slight disagreement was over, they were friends again. They continued to be teacher and pupil. I went and

sat with them when I had finished my work. I thought of them both as my children in some ways. I had been proud of Cathy for a long time. And now, I was sure Hareton would soon be someone to be proud of. I could hardly recognize the interested, intelligent looking person in front of me as   5
the boy I had seen here before. I remembered the day I had found my little lady, when she had ridden out of the Grange pretending to be an Arab trader.

Heathcliff came in unexpectedly, and the two friends lifted their eyes together, to look at him. Their eyes are exactly the   10
same, and they are those of Catherine Earnshaw. I suppose it was this fact that upset Heathcliff. He walked over to them, took the book Hareton had been learning from, looked at it, then returned it, saying nothing. He sent them both away, then, and I was about to go too, when he told me to stay   15
where I was.

Heathcliff is changing

'It is a poor ending, isn't it?' he said. 'A poor ending to all my efforts. My old enemies have almost beaten me. I could still destroy them, through those two. I could do, and no one could stop me. But what is the use? I can't take the trouble.   20
That may sound like kindness, but it's not. I have lost the ability to enjoy destruction, and I'm too idle to destroy for nothing.

'Nelly, there is a strange change approaching. I hardly remember to eat and drink. Those two who have left the room   25
are the only objects that still mean anything to me. I won't speak about her, and don't want to even think about her. He is different. His likeness to my Cathy makes me think of her all the time. I cannot look at anything, even this floor, without seeing her face on it. In every cloud, in every tree, filling   30
the air at night and every object during the day. I am surrounded by her. The entire world is a dreadful collection of memories showing that she was here once, and that I have lost her. Hareton's face is the ghost of my Cathy.'

He began to walk up and down the room, muttering terrible things to himself. I wondered how it would end.   35

20   The End of Heathcliff

For some days after that evening we did not see Heathcliff at meal-times.

One night, after the family were all in bed, I heard him go out. In the morning I found that he was still away. We were
5 in April then, and the apple trees near the south wall were in flower. After breakfast Cathy insisted that I sat under the trees at the end of the house. Hareton dug her little garden, which they had moved to that corner after Joseph had complained. My young lady, who had run down near the gate to
10 find some flowers, returned and told us that Mr Heathcliff was coming in.

'And he spoke to me,' she added. 'He told me to go away, but he looked so different from his normal self that I stopped to stare at him. He looked so excited, wild and glad!'
15 'Night-walking amuses him, then,' I said. I went inside to greet the master. He stood at the open door. He was pale, yet he had a strange joyful look in his eye that changed his face completely.

'I don't think it right to wander outside,' I said, 'instead of
20 being in bed. I expect you'll catch a bad cold or fever. You will be ill.'

'It's nothing,' he answered. 'Now leave me alone, and don't annoy me.'

I obeyed, but as I passed him I noticed that he was
25 breathing very fast.

'Yes,' I thought to myself, 'he is ill. I wonder what he's been doing.'

That lunch-time he sat down to eat with us, but got up again and did not touch his food. We saw him walking up and
30 down the garden.

After an hour or two, he returned. I asked him what it was that bothered him.

'Why do you look so odd. Where were you last night? I'm not asking you through idle curiosity — '

'You are questioning me through very idle curiosity,' he interrupted with a laugh. 'But I'll answer. Last night I was on the edge of hell. Today I am within sight of my heaven. I can see it, it is so close. And now you'd better go. You'll neither see nor hear anything to frighten you, if you don't interfere.'

Next morning I made breakfast for the household, as I usually did. Hareton and Catherine liked to have theirs outside under the trees, and I put a little table out there for them.

Heathcliff's visions

When I came back inside I found Heathcliff. After talking to Joseph about some farm business, he took his seat. I gave him some coffee, but he took no notice of it. He was staring at the opposite wall with restless eyes. He even appeared to stop breathing for about half a minute, he was so interested in what he saw.

'Come now,' I said, 'drink your coffee while it's hot.' He still took no notice.

'Master!' I cried. 'Stop staring like that!'

'Don't shout,' he replied. 'Tell me, are we alone?'

'Of course we are,' I answered.

He then cleared the table in front of him, so that he could rest his arms on it. He leant forward. Now I noticed that he was not looking at the wall. He was looking at something within a few yards.

At last he got up and left the house. The hours crept by. He returned after midnight, and instead of going to bed, shut himself in a room below. I listened to him, walking up and down, and finally dressed and went down to him.

He was muttering to himself. The only words I could understand was the name of Catherine, joined to some wild terms of love or suffering. He heard me, and said, 'Nelly, come here. Is it morning?'

'It's nearly four o'clock,' I answered. 'I'll get you a candle, and you can go upstairs.'

'No, I don't want to go upstairs,' he said. 'I want you to light the fire here.'

While I started to do what he ordered, he continued walking up and down.

5   'You must rest,' I said, 'and eat. You have become very thin and weak.'

'It's not my fault I cannot eat nor rest,' he replied.

'If you go on like this,' I said, 'you will die.'

The death of Heathcliff

As soon as he heard the other members of the household
10 getting up, he did go up to his room, and I breathed more easily. In the afternoon, he came into the kitchen again. The following evening, I saw that his window was swinging open and the rain was coming in. I rushed up and pushed the door open. He was lying on the bed. His face and throat were
15 washed with rain, and the bed-clothes dripped, and he was perfectly still. I closed the window. Then I turned to him. I combed his long black hair and tried to close his black staring eyes. They would not shut. I cried out to Joseph, but he refused to help.

20   'The devil's taken his soul,' he cried. 'What a wicked man he looks, staring at death!'

Dr Kenneth was called, but he was unable to say exactly why the master had died. I did not say anything about the fact that he had not eaten for several days, fearing that it
25 might lead to trouble.

We buried him as he had wished, next to Catherine Linton. I hope he sleeps well. But the country people, if you ask them, swear that he walks. Stupid tales, I'm sure.

Hareton and Cathy are to be married on New Year's Day.
30 It will be 1803 then, and they will come to the Grange to live, and I will go with them. Joseph will be left to take care of Wuthering Heights.

There are three gravestones on the churchyard slope next to the moor. The middle one is grey, and half buried in the

grass. Grass is creeping up the foot of Edgar Linton's. Heathcliff's is still bare. The birds sing among the wild flowers on
the moor, and the soft wind breathes through the grass. How
can anyone imagine unquiet rest for the sleepers in that quiet
5 earth?

Questions

Chapter   6   1. Describe the conditions at Thrushcross Grange when Cathy was first married.
              2. How did Cathy feel when Heathcliff returned?
              3. Describe Heathcliff.
              4. Why did Heathcliff go and live at Wuthering Heights?
              5. What had happened to Isabella, and why was Edgar so upset?

Chapter   7   1. Describe, in your own words, Ellen's return to the Heights, and what she found there.
              2. Why did Catherine become ill?
              3. Why didn't Ellen believe at first that Catherine was ill?

Chapter   8   1. Describe Catherine's illness.
              2. Why did Catherine believe Ellen to be her secret enemy?
              3. What did the doctor do when he saw Catherine's illness?
              4. What did Isabella do?

Chapter   9   1. Give examples to show that Catherine thought she would not live long.
              2. Why was Isabella's letter to Ellen 'odd'?
              3. Describe Isabella's arrival at Wuthering Heights.
              4. Why did Hindley frighten Isabella?
              5. Describe Joseph and Hareton.

Chapter   10 1. What happened after Ellen had read Isabella's letter?
              2. Describe how Ellen found Heathcliff and Isabella when she went to the Heights.
              3. Describe Heathcliff's behaviour towards his wife.
              4. What did Heathcliff persuade Ellen to do for him?

Chapter   11 1. In your own words, describe Catherine's appearance after her illness.
              2. What was the importance of Edgar being at church?
              3. Why did Catherine say she wanted to die?
              4. Explain the following: 'I love my murderer. But how can I love yours?'
              5. What happened when Edgar returned?

Chapter 12   1. Why did Isabella leave the Heights?
2. Describe in your own words how Hindley tried to kill Heathcliff.
3. Explain the following: 'Catherine used to boast that she stood between you and bodily harm.'
4. What happened to Isabella after she left?

Chapter 13   1. Describe, in your own words, Hindley Earnshaw's death.
2. How did Heathcliff come to be master at Wuthering Heights?
3. How did Heathcliff treat Hareton, and why did he treat him like this?
4. Describe the child, Cathy.
5. Why did Edgar Linton take a journey away from Thrushcross Grange?
6. Tell how Cathy tricked Ellen into letting her go out.
7. Where did Ellen finally find Cathy?

Chapter 14   1. Who was Linton, and why did he come to the Grange?
2. Explain the following: 'Our fears were soon to come true . . . '
3. Describe Heathcliff's feelings about his son.
4. Why did Heathcliff intend to look after Linton well?

Chapter 15   1. Describe in your own words, how Cathy met her cousin Linton.
2. Give your opinion of Linton.
3. Why did Cathy tell her father of her visit to Wuthering Heights?
4. What did Cathy do after she had been forbidden to see Linton?
5. How did Nelly discover what was happening, and how did she stop it?

Chapter 16   1. Explain the following: 'Poor Cathy was troubled by Heathcliff's words . . . '
2. What happened when they went to the Heights?
3. How did Cathy manage to visit Linton with no one at the Grange knowing?

Chapter 17 1. How did Ellen discover what had happened?
               2. How did Heathcliff manage to succeed in his plan to trap Ellen and Cathy in Wuthering Heights?
               3. Why did he do so?
               4. Why could they not escape?

Chapter 18 1. What happened to Ellen, and who rescued her?
               2. How did Cathy manage to escape?
               3. Why did Heathcliff come to Thrushcross Grange after Mr Linton died?
               4. Describe what you think the new Mrs Heathcliff's life must have been like at the Heights.

Chapter 19 1. Why did Ellen return to Wuthering Heights?
               2. Why did Cathy finally decide to make a friend of Hareton?
               3. What were the results of that friendship for Hareton?
               4. Describe, in your own words, what they did to the garden, and how Joseph behaved afterwards.
               5. How did Cathy make Heathcliff so angry at breakfast?

Chapter 20 1. Describe, in your own words, what you think was happening to Heathcliff.
               2. How did Joseph feel about Heathcliff's death?
               3. Describe, in your own words, how you imagine the church and graves in Gimmerton churchyard to look.

OXFORD PROGRESSIVE ENGLISH READERS

GRADE 1

Vocabulary restricted to 1900 head words
Illustrated in two and partly in full colours
One illustration every 6 pages on average

The Adventures of Hang Tuah	MUBIN SHEPPARD
Alice's Adventures in Wonderland	LEWIS CARROLL
A Christmas Carol	CHARLES DICKENS
Don Quixote	CERVANTES
Great Expectations	CHARLES DICKENS
Gulliver's Travels	JONATHAN SWIFT
The House of Sixty Fathers	MEINDERT DEJONG
Islands in the Sky	ARTHUR C. CLARKE
Jane Eyre	CHARLOTTE BRONTË
Little Women	LOUISA M. ALCOTT
Madam White Snake	RETOLD BY BENJAMIN CHIA
Oliver Twist	CHARLES DICKENS
Plays for Malaysian Schools I	PATRICK YEOH
The Stone Junk	RETOLD BY D.H. HOWE
Stories of Shakespeare's Plays I	RETOLD BY N. KATES
The Tale of the Bounty	RETOLD BY H.G. WYATT
Tales from Tolstoy	RETOLD BY R.D. BINFIELD
Tales of Si Kabayan	MURTAGH MURPHY
The Talking Tree & Other Stories	DAVID McROBBIE
The Tiger of Lembah Pahit	NORMA R. YOUNGBERG
A Time of Darkness	SHAMUS FRAZER
Treasure Island	R.L. STEVENSON

GRADE 2

Vocabulary restricted to 2900 head words
One two-coloured illustration every 10 pages on average

The Adventures of Tom Sawyer	MARK TWAIN
Around the World in Eighty Days	JULES VERNE
Asia Pacific Stories	MURTAGH MURPHY
Beau Geste	P.C. WREN
Chinese Tales of the Supernatural	RETOLD BY BENJAMIN CHIA
The Crocodile Dies Twice	SHAMUS FRAZER
David Copperfield	CHARLES DICKENS
Five Tales	OSCAR WILDE
The Hound of the Baskervilles	SIR ARTHUR CONAN DOYLE
The Missing Scientist	S.F. STEVENS
Plays for Malaysian Schools II	PATRICK YEOH
Robinson Crusoe	DANIEL DEFOE
Seven Chinese Stories	T.J. SHERIDAN
Stories of Shakespeare's Plays II	RETOLD BY WYATT & FULLERTON
A Tale of Two Cities	CHARLES DICKENS
Tales of Crime & Detection	RETOLD BY G.F. WEAR
Two Famous English Comedies	RETOLD BY RICHARD CROFT
Vanity Fair	W.M. THACKERAY

GRADE 3

Vocabulary restricted to 3500 head words
One two-coloured illustration every 15 pages on average

Animal Farm	GEORGE ORWELL
Battle of Wits at Crimson Cliff	RETOLD BY BENJAMIN CHIA
Dr Jekyll & Mr Hyde & Other Stories	R.L. STEVENSON
From Russia, with Love	IAN FLEMING
The Gifts & Other Stories	O. HENRY & OTHERS
Journey to the Centre of the Earth	JULES VERNE
Kidnapped	R.L. STEVENSON
King Solomon's Mines	H. RIDER HAGGARD
Lady Precious Stream	S.I. HSIUNG
The Light of Day	ERIC AMBLER
The Mask of Dimitrios	ERIC AMBLER
Moonraker	IAN FLEMING
The Moonstone	WILKIE COLLINS
A Night of Terror & Other Strange Tales	GUY DE MAUPASSANT
The Red Winds	SHAMUS FRAZER
Seven Stories	H.G. WELLS
Stories of Shakespeare's Plays III	RETOLD BY H.G. WYATT
Tales of Mystery & Imagination	EDGAR ALLAN POE
The War of the Worlds	H.G. WELLS
20,000 Leagues under the Sea	JULES VERNE
The Woman in White	WILKIE COLLINS
Wuthering Heights	EMILY BRONTË
You Only Live Twice	IAN FLEMING

GRADE 4

Vocabulary restricted to 5000 head words
One two-coloured illustration every 15 pages on average

Frankenstein	MARY SHELLEY
The Mayor of Casterbridge	THOMAS HARDY
Pride and Prejudice	JANE AUSTEN